SHOP CLASS HALL PASS

SHOP CLASS HALL PASS

Facing the Buried Trauma of Sexual Assault

Karin Martel

EDITIONS

Cover design by Doowah Design.
Photo of Karin Martel by Betty Weller.

This book was printed on Ancient Forest Friendly paper.
Printed and bound in Canada by Hignell Book Printing Inc.

We acknowledge the support of the Canada Council for the Arts and the Manitoba Arts Council for our publishing program.

Library and Archives Canada Cataloguing in Publication

Title: Shop class hall pass : facing the buried trauma of sexual assault / Karin Martel.
Names: Martel, Karin, author.
Identifiers: Canadiana (print) 20220430039 |
Canadiana (ebook) 20220430063 |
ISBN 9781773241180 (softcover) |
ISBN 9781773241197 (EPUB)
Subjects: LCSH: Martel, Karin. |
Subjects: LCSH: Martel, Karin. |
LCSH: Rape victims—Saskatchewan—Biography. |
LCSH: Post-traumatic stress disorder—Patients—Saskatchewan—Biography. | LCGFT: Autobiographies.
Classification: LCC HV6569.C32 S27 2022 |
DDC 362.88392092—dc23

Signature Editions
P.O. Box 206, RPO Corydon, Winnipeg, Manitoba, R3M 3S7
www.signature-editions.com

For 1984–2018 Karin and all the people with stories like her who need to hear that what happened to them mattered and healing is possible.

1

'd meant to cancel the appointment to see my therapist, Val, because I'd been feeling much better. I use the term *my therapist* loosely as I'd only seen her three times two years ago in the late fall of 2016. A few months previous, I began having little episodes. I'd suddenly be arrested by a gust of terror and get the same feeling I have when I am plummeting to my death in a dream only to wake at the last minute. First, my heart would seize like a failed car engine, then burst into a pounding frenzy, while my chest and back muscles tensed around my lungs like a ropy python squeezing its prey. The harder I tried to pull oxygen into my lungs, the tighter the python wound. The feeling wasn't unusual. I feel like that often, but it is always tied to something else: meeting a friend, going to an appointment, making a non-work-related phone call… you know, regular nerves. So, the problem wasn't that I felt that way, it was that there didn't seem to be a reason for it. And so there I'd be, reading a book, drying my hair, folding clothes, and a gush of dread would wash over me, making me feel like something bad was going to happen. It didn't make sense because my life was practically worry-free.

I was in the twenty-third year of a happy marriage with my loving and supportive husband, Jeff. We had our two healthy adult children, Maddie and Max, living with us, going to university, destined to graduate debt-free. We owned our house, had accumulated a safety net of savings and had no debt. I had a secure job with the city. I didn't have any health problems. On top of that, I did everything I could think of to lead a *balanced* life. I did yoga, meditated, decluttered, simplified, exercised, ate a healthy diet, drank little caffeine and less alcohol. I've read extensively in the genre of self-help. I didn't feel my life warranted getting these waves of unease that came out of nowhere. So, I thought it must be work-related.

I'm a Special Constable in Communications at the Saskatoon Police Service. My job involves answering the non-emergency police line and 911, as well as dispatching officers. Recent studies have shown that emergency service call takers and dispatchers can suffer PTSD symptoms from indirect exposure to traumatic events. I didn't think I had PTSD, but at the time, I was in my eighth year and considered that maybe my job was the reason for my unexplained episodes. So, I went to see Val. It felt good to talk to her but I can't say we pinned down any particular issue and addressed it. Still, talking seemed to help and after three sessions I hadn't felt like I needed to go back, until now.

I'm the only one in the waiting room. I can feel the brisk November chill pressing through the wall behind me and brushing past my neck. Nature pictures adorn the walls. A few colourful fish swim in a softly bubbling aquarium and easy-listening tunes waft through the room. A stack of magazines lies on a table to my right. I'm tempted to pick one up, but I'm not sure which magazine is the *right* one to read in the waiting room of a therapist's office. I don't know what kind of message it will send if Val catches me browsing through the holiday edition of *House and Home*. So instead of risking Val, or another therapist catching me flipping through the *wrong* magazine, I turn my attention to a small bookshelf on my left lined with children's books and toys. I wonder why there are children's books and toys in the waiting room of a therapist's office and then cringe. I shouldn't be here. Nothing bad has ever happened to me. Certainly not *children-needing-to-see-a-therapist* bad. When I called in early October to make an appointment, Val's first available time was a month away. A month filled with her helping people with real problems. Not someone like me who has a great life and can't take a little stress. I feel like I'm wasting my time, and hers.

I feel a twitch building in my neck. I try to resist it but a little one sneaks through as the vertebra at the base of my skull crunches in a tiny backwards half circle taking my head with it. My neck isn't satisfied with the little twitch and, as I try to resist a big one, my right shoulder shoots up as my neck jerks my head towards it and then takes my head on a larger half backwards circle until it meets my left shoulder. Even though I know I'm the only one in the waiting room, I look around to see if anyone saw. Maybe someone snuck up the stairs and is peeking at me, or someone cracked open a door and is watching. No one is. After the twitch comes the ribbit. My lower jaw juts forward and up as the muscles in my throat push out the skin under my chin until I look like a frog mid-croak. I press my lips together to prevent the cycle from completing itself, but my jaws burst apart as wide as they can go as my lips stretch around my teeth, giving me the appearance of the tortured man in Edvard Munch's *The Scream*. My body has done this little performance, its Martha Graham interpretive dance of stress, for as long as I can remember. I try telling myself there is no reason to be nervous, that I want to be here, that Val is kind.

I try to relax my muscles by attempting a tactical breathing technique I learned at a work training day. It involves breathing in slowly for four counts, holding for four counts and breathing out for four counts. I get to number two on my in-breath and the python around my lungs wakes up and tightens its grip. I try to breathe into my belly, but I end up just forcing my stomach muscles out without taking in more air. When I hold for four counts my heart pounds frantically against my sternum. I give up. I wish I could take deep breaths. I try every now and then because I've heard it's supposed to be helpful to calm down, but it just doesn't work for me. I think it must be because of the way my chest or diaphragm are shaped.

I fidget with my clothing. I'm wearing a dark T-shirt and a dark cardigan. Both are made of wicking fabric, the only kind of fabric I wear because of my faucet-like armpits, which have already drenched my clothing. I put my hands on my hips and splay out my elbows to let air circulate under my arms. I take a surreptitious sniff, trying to make it look like I am just scratching my nose with my shoulder in case anyone is looking. I try not to think about the sweat pooling around my groin. I hope I don't leave a mark on the chair. My shoulders, neck and face take their cue. *And five, six, seven, eight: Twitch*, my neck yanks my head back, *ribbit*, my chin and neck push out, *stretch*, my jaw wrenches open.

I run my fingers through my hair, making sure it's still okay. I had a pixie cut the last time I was here. It was a last-minute decision before I went on a work trip and I've been trying to grow it out ever since, which is hard because I tend to get my hair cut when I feel stressed. When I first met Jeff, I had thick, dark blonde hair that fell in natural waves around my shoulders. Six months later, after moving from the American Midwest to Saskatoon and right before we got married, I had a hairdresser chop it all off into something suspiciously resembling a bowl cut, which made me look like a button mushroom in our wedding photos. Now, despite making repeated vows not to cut my hair, but having it done anyway, it's finally grown into a chin-length bob. I remember in one of our sessions telling Val about how much I worry about my hair. What a stupid thing to talk to a therapist about. Like Val has time for hair worries. *Twitch. Ribbit. Stretch.*

Val comes out of her office and greets me. Like me, she's in her late forties. She has short wavy dark hair, creamy skin and a friendly energy. She smiles warmly, comments on the cold, grey November day, and welcomes me into her office: a cozy room decorated in earth tones and filled with furniture, a couch with throw pillows, an armchair, her desk and office chair, and a bookshelf neatly lined with evidence of her knowledge. On the wall hang a clock and various artworks, including a large, square, lightly stained wooden piece with an organic shape painted on it. Side tables hold interesting knickknacks clients can play with: a smooth stone to rub and a small cube with buttons to click, slide and flip. I sit on the thickly cushioned couch. She sits on her desk chair, grabs my file and swivels to face me.

"So, it's been a while since we last saw each other," she says, as she pages through my file. "How have you been doing?"

I go into my *let's impress my therapist with how much of a self-aware and balanced person I am* spiel. "Things are going really good." I rub my cold sweaty palms along my thighs. "There've been some changes at work so that's been good. Our team is all getting along really well. I get a little nervous going into work sometimes, but I still love my job."

Val nods and makes a note.

"And about a year and a half ago I started working on my body image, eating and weight issues, which has been almost a lifetime worry for me and it's really paid off. I spend way less time obsessing about what I eat and how much I weigh."

Val smiles, says a few encouraging things, and makes a few more jots on her notepad. I feel like I've said enough to let her know how fine I really am. So that when I tell her my concerns, she knows I have perspective, that in the big scheme of things I know I'm fortunate and that I realize I don't have problems like other people. Like the kids who play with the toys in the waiting room.

"So, I made this appointment because for the last month or so I felt like I was coming down with something. I would wake up with a sore throat but it never turned into a cold. I ached all over. I was lethargic and had trouble concentrating. I really felt off my game at work, like I just couldn't get it together. I felt like calling in sick to work almost every day, but never did. I lost interest in exercising and a dance class Jeff and I were taking. And I had this constant tightness and heaviness in my chest. I'd had pneumonia three times before, so I thought it might be that, but I never developed any other symptoms. After a few weeks of this, I thought it might be because of work stress so that's why I made the appointment with you."

Val adjusts her glasses and gently tilts her head to the side like a cat who hears a curious sound.

"But in the last three days I've been feeling much better and almost cancelled the appointment, but I kept it because there are a couple of calls from work that have been kind of bothering me, and I thought you could help me make a plan to deal with them and future calls."

Val raises her eyebrows in acknowledgement and writes a few more notes.

"And there is this other life event that's been on my mind, something that happened in high school," I add.

"Life event?" Val looks up sharply. "I don't remember you mentioning a life event before." She riffles through her notes.

Life event? Where did that phrase come from? It was more of a *nothing event* that doesn't have anything to do with how I've been feeling now, and not what I came here to talk about. If I tell her the story, I'm going to sound whiny, dramatic. What I really should talk about are the calls.

One of the calls was from two years earlier. A young man called 911 and yelled that he was trapped under a piece of industrial equipment, he yelled out the name of the business. He was alone, sounded scared, and screamed he was going to die. He lost consciousness while I was still on the line with him. I often think about that call. I can still hear the desperation in his voice, his helplessness. I feel mine. I never knew what happened to him until recently when I finally had the chance to ask the outcome. For the last two years, the man, my son's age now, had been trapped in my mind, partly crushed, all by himself and believing he was going to die. And for two years of not knowing, he existed both rescued, healed and reunited with his family, or dead with grieving parents who never had a chance to say goodbye. When I learned the man had died, I burst into tears.

The second call was a brother reporting his sister missing because she hadn't been in contact, which wasn't like her. There was something in his voice that I couldn't quite place. He didn't sound very worried and it seemed like he was hiding something, which made me drill him with questions to see if there was more to the story. I took the report and asked him to please call us back if and when she contacted him. He agreed, sounding relieved that I thought she would eventually call or text him. And I did think that, because that is how the majority of missing persons calls turn out. When I heard the relief in his voice, I finally figured out what he was trying to hide: how worried he actually was. Later that evening while dispatching, a call came in: a woman's body had been found. I feared it was the man's sister. It was. Because of the circumstances surrounding her death, I knew there wasn't anything I could have done to save her. But that didn't change the fact that the call, the voice of the concerned brother, and the events of that night replayed through my mind regularly.

I've had numerous calls dealing with death, tragedy, people taken too soon, too abruptly, too violently. Dying alone and afraid. But these two calls stuck with me and I wanted help letting them go.

"Well," Val says, "you're in the lead. You can start with either of the calls or this life event."

I inwardly cringe when she says *life event*. But I'm impressed by how she says it so sincerely and without a trace of condescension. Still, there is no way I'm going to start with that. It's the calls that are important.

"I'll start with the life event."

What am I doing?

Val nods and waits for me to begin. I don't even have to begin. This is my therapy session. I'm in the lead. I can change my mind. But I've already started, so might as well get it over with. It's no big deal. I'll tell my story. Val is too professional to roll her eyes at my teenage drama. She'll be empathetic and validate it. We'll wrap it up into a nice little package and put it on the shelf. It'll take five minutes. Then we can move on to the important stuff.

I lean a little forward in my seat. "Okay, it happened when I was fourteen," I begin, with a breezy tone of voice to match the triteness of the story. "And I haven't thought about it very much since. But lately I've been thinking about it a lot more. Maybe because I've been watching too much news about Brett Kavanaugh and Christine Blasey Ford, you know, how he has been nominated for the Supreme Court and she has come forward with allegations that he sexually assaulted her when they were teenagers."

Val puts her pen down and looks up at me, her eyes slightly widening.

"Anyway, it was ninth grade and I was the only girl in the metal shop class. I think it started on the first day, but I can't be sure. We were all in a group standing near some of the machinery while the teacher was talking to us about safety or something when this boy came up behind me and grabbed me in kind of a bear hug. I tried to get out of his grip, but he was too strong for me. As I was struggling and yelling at him to let me go, everyone, including the teacher, was looking at us. Then he started grabbing my breasts, my butt and my crotch. Everyone was watching me trying to get away from him, but no one did anything. He let me go when he was done with me. I've always remembered it as happening every day but I can't be sure it did. I do know it happened a lot. Regularly. Sometimes he invited the other boys to feel me up too. Sometimes they did. It happened in the hallway in between classes too. I begged the teacher to get the boy to stop, but the teacher never helped me."

I lean back and try and act as normal as possible, hoping she doesn't notice I'm vibrating. I try to keep my neck and throat in check, keep my face neutral. I don't want her to think I'm a big baby who gets shook up telling a story about something that happened over thirty years ago.

Val squares herself towards me, straightens her spine and lowers her chin slightly. She's not smiling, she's not nodding. Instead, she's looking directly at me, making sure I'm looking at her, making sure I'm listening as she begins to list off words and phrases like *violation, intrusion, violence, betrayal of trust.*

Part of me thinks Val is being overly dramatic and tries to hold back the tears welling up in my eyes. Another part of me lets some of the tears fall and says "thank you" over and over. I'm surprised at the relief I feel that she didn't dismiss my story out of hand. That even though it happened such a long time ago and isn't relevant to my life now, it doesn't mean I'm foolish for bringing it up.

She finishes listing adjectives and we sit in silence for a moment while I wait for her to ask me about my work calls. Instead, she swivels towards her bookshelf, picks out a large well-worn paperback held together by a rubber band which she snaps off. In between the covers of the book are bundles of pages held together with paper clips. She flips through the bundles until she finds the one she's looking for. She removes the paper clip and starts asking me questions.

"Do you find that you are overly alert for danger?"

"What?" I furrow my brow, caught off guard by the unrelated question.

"For instance, when you go somewhere, even here, does it matter where you decide to sit? Some people feel safer if they can see the door and have an easy way out of the room."

I think about where I'm sitting, on the end of the couch immediately opposite the door, nothing in my way. Val is off to the right in front of me. I feel I could make it to the door before she does if I get a fraction of a head start. It also allows me to keep an eye on it in case anyone tries to enter. I sat in this same spot the last three times. It's not by coincidence or chance. When I go into a room, any room, I consider all of these things before I pick a seat. I prefer my back to a wall, but not a wall with an open window. I prefer to be on either end of a couch, bench or row, but not in the middle. All these little deliberations go through my mind every time I enter a room because my neck, throat and mouth will betray me all the more if I pick the wrong spot. But I don't see what it has to do with anything. Doesn't everyone do that?

I nod.

"Do you ever feel spaced out?"

I must look confused again because she gives an example.

"Like you feel not present or cut off. Some people may feel clumsy or walk into walls or furniture because of it."

I still don't know why she is asking me these questions, but I know exactly what she means. "Yeah, I feel spaced out a lot. Like most of the time I feel like I live in the space in my skull just between my eyebrows and the top of my head, and lots of the time I feel like I'm up here," I hold my hand just above my head, "and my body is on autopilot." The effect of it is that the majority of my life feels like I've been driving after a night shift and, after I'm parked at home, I can't remember how I got there. But what does this have to do with anything? What is going on? Why is she asking me this stuff?

"I'm sorry, what does this have to do with anything?"

"These are questions from this book." She shows me the book's cover: *The Courage to Heal: A Guide for Women Survivors of Child Sexual Abuse.*

Now I'm really lost, because I wasn't sexually abused, much less sexually abused as a child. I start to shake my head. Val's got this all wrong.

"No, that's not me, it never bothered me. It doesn't have anything to do with that stuff." I shake my head furiously at the idea.

"Karin." Val presses her lips together into a grave line and leans towards me. "When you were telling me about what happened, I noticed a few things. I could tell that your heart rate increased and your mouth went dry. Are you sweating?"

I nod as my eyes travel from one armpit to the other, acknowledging the cold damp clothing under each. *Thanks for noticing, Val.*

"I've also noticed that you are a shallow breather, does that sound right?"

"Yeah. I mean, I can take a deep breath, but when I do it feels like there is a belt tightening around my rib cage."

Wait. Is that not normal?

"These symptoms that you have, sweating, dry mouth, and increasing heart rate, are all associated with the threat response. When we are threatened, our fear centre in our amygdala is activated." Val points to a spot behind her ear. "When our amygdala is activated, we have a biological response that prepares us to fight or flee or freeze."

I nod, letting her know I understand the principle of what she is saying but still not seeing what this has to do with anything. I was never physically hurt. I wasn't in a life-or-death situation.

"This threat response would have been triggered every time that boy grabbed you, and now, when you tell the story, it was triggered again. When this happens over and over, and you said it happened regularly, then the amygdala can get sensitive and misinterpret some situations as being more dangerous."

My head keeps bobbing politely while the rest of me waits for her to finish so I can tell her about the calls.

"When we start interpreting safe situations as being dangerous, we often unconsciously develop ways of coping by doing things we think will keep us safe. So, the questions I'm asking are helping me determine if and how much this has affected you."

"It hasn't affected me at all." My hands splay out in a *how aren't you getting this?* motion. I don't know how to make myself any clearer.

Val takes a deep breath and looks through her notes of our past meetings. "Okay, what about your thoughts of suicide?"

"That has nothing to do with this." I wave my hands in front of me, attempting to dispel her concern. "I mean I have suicidal thoughts all the time, but they aren't a problem. I made a decision a long time ago that I wasn't going to kill myself and since then, whenever I have suicidal thoughts, I just remind myself that I already made a decision about that, and the impulse eventually passes."

"Okay." Val twists her face in thought, like she is trying to work out how to explain the internet to an Amish grandmother.

"It sounds like you have a strategy for dealing with suicidal thoughts. Can you tell me when they began?"

I shrug my shoulders. I can't believe she is still talking about this. I already told her it's not a problem.

She flips through the pages of my file. "In one of our sessions, you talked about your suicide attempt. Can you tell me when that was?"

I look up at the ceiling trying to remember. "Either the summer after ninth or tenth grade."

"That makes sense."

"No, no, that didn't have anything to do with it." I shake my head and again attempt to wave this whole line of reasoning, this whole conversation, away with my hands. "That had to do with me being bipolar."

Val gives a little sigh and places the palms of her hands together and explains how there may be links between childhood trauma and bipolar disorder. How a person may have a predisposition to being bipolar and then a traumatic incident can be a catalyst.

Something inside me jolts to understanding. Like I've been mindlessly eating a hamburger at my neighbour's barbecue when the host informs me it's really my pet cat, Rosie, I'm chewing on.

I grip my knees with my cold sweaty hands and lean forward towards Val. "Are you telling me, the reason I'm bipolar is because of that?"

"It's a risk factor and it could be a possibility." Val crosses her legs.

And just like that, the world drops out from under me. My stomach lurches into my throat, my heart jumps into a wild beat, and everything goes dark as I plummet into nothingness.

I lean back against the couch and let it support me while my insides collapse. Val keeps talking to me but I'm not there. My mind hit the autopilot switch and ejected before Val even crossed her legs. I know I look normal, like I'm listening, because I'm good at looking normal. But inside I'm too busy hurtling to my death to pay attention to what she is saying. I need to get out of here *right now!* But I don't move. I can't move. Not till she tells me I can go. Now she is talking about the pages in her hand. She's asking me something. Something about the pages. She wants to know if I would like to borrow the pages about the different ways people cope. There's no way I want those pages.

"Yes, please." *What the hell?*

Val swivels around in her chair to tap the bundle of pages on her desk so they can be neatly paperclipped back together while I stay trapped on the couch, wondering what just happened. Val turns back around and hands the pages to me. I want to swat them away.

"Thank you." I shove them into my purse without looking at them.

"You might find that you aren't ready yet to look at them right now."

I'm not looking at them ever.

"Or even at all, and that's okay. It's okay to go slowly and be gentle with yourself. Take all the time you need."

"Okay."

"Would you like to schedule an appointment?"

No, let's not ever do this again.

"Yes, please."

Oh my god, oh my god, oh my god.

She schedules an appointment for her next available time, four weeks away. She repeats how if the pages are triggering that it's okay to stop reading them. To take a break, rest, distract myself. We say our goodbyes and I leave her office.

My mouth is dry and I'm soaked in sweat. I feel faint and a hundred miles away from my body as I fumble with my coat in the waiting room while forcing my face into a smile to show the receptionist: I had a pleasant visit with Val. Violent shivers begin to course through my body before I even step out into the biting cold air. My body walks to the car while my mind flails around as I plunge further into the dark abyss. I need to do something to stop it. I need something to ground me. I know exactly what to do. I get in my car and drive to the mall, all the while telling myself I'm in no condition to drive. My body ignores me; it needs to get rid of this feeling and it knows shopping usually does the trick. Driving to the mall I resist the urge to swerve into oncoming traffic, mostly because a traffic accident isn't a guaranteed suicide. Plus, I don't want to take anyone with me. I try to take a deep breath, but the python wakes up and tenaciously grips my lungs.

After parking, I take the escalator from the exhaust-filled underground parking garage up into the bright lights of the mall. I will myself not to take the steps two at a time, to walk instead of running through the throng of shoppers ambling along. I finally make it to my destination, walk through the entrance of the Eddie Bauer store and force my body and face to look normal, while inside I'm still tumbling ass-over-tea-kettle into the void.

A friendly staff member greets me. Most of the staff know me because I shop here almost weekly. Let me clarify: I come here almost weekly, try on clothes but don't always buy something. I'm embarrassed about how often I'm here. Today is no different. I wander around, trying to find a rack of clothing to land on that will lure my brain back into my body, hoping the staff doesn't remember me being here last week, and trying not to think about pages in my purse. Trying not to think at all.

I'm not really looking at anything. I don't have to. I don't just come in regularly, I also scour their website daily, scrolling through their new arrivals and sales. I know their stock by heart. I know I've already bought all the *acceptable* items from their current collection. I pretend to be interested in a rack of multi-coloured flannel shirts and a display of fleece pullovers, looking for something to grab onto to stop the fall. But it's not working and I start to panic that this time I won't be able to find a handhold, that a ledge won't appear, that this hole is too deep. And even if I am able to grasp onto something and avoid a fatal *kersplat* that I'll be too far gone, my mind won't be able to find its way back to the rest of me.

I leave the store and try to think which of my other regular retail haunts might help, but something inside me, the something that made the appointment, that told the story, that took the pages, tells me that shopping isn't going to fix it this time. Tells me to leave.

I relent, drive home, park on the street, and stare at my little bungalow with the terra-cotta-coloured stucco and rogue cotoneaster growing next to the chipped concrete steps. I'm not ready to go in. I'm not ready to take this feeling into my home, our home: it's not welcome to tread our sixty-year-old scratched and stained hardwood floors. I don't want it to take a seat at the large dining room table, protected by decades of lemon-scented Pledge, that I inherited from my nana. I don't want the feeling to follow me into my room, my sanctuary with my twin bed topped with a thick rose-patterned duvet and a stack of Jane Austen and Connie Willis books on the maple bedside table.

The steely cold of November seeps into the car, turning my breath into fog as I stare at my house. And then I see movement. A small dark figure slinks around the corner of the house and sidles up next to the car. It's Maddie's petite brown tabby cat, Rosie, scolding me to let her into the house. I sigh, get out of the car, usher Rosie into the house, go to my room, throw the vile pages into my dresser drawer, fall onto my bed and begin to cry.

2

Allow me to backtrack. When I say my life is fine, what I really mean is that from all observable indicators, my life looks fine, and I have no reason to complain. But my inner life? That's a different story. Starting sometime in high school, I knew that something wasn't quite right with me. I had these *moods*. Euphoric highs in which I felt interconnected with everyone and everything. There was no end to my intelligence, my understanding, my abilities. I was funny and fun, loving and loved. Everything I thought and said was clever and insightful. No one else in the world could possibly be as special as me. But then the high worked its way into a fit of agitation and I would crash. And in the low I could not name a more stupid and dull, hated and loathsome person than me. Every utterance I made was odious, every action reprehensible. I believed I didn't deserve love, friendship, or even tolerance.

Most people didn't notice my moods because I burned through friends too quickly for them to catch on to it. But I did. And shortly after we were married, so did Jeff. He used to call it the Karin roller coaster. In the midst of a mood swing he would raise his hands over his head like he was on a roller coaster racing downwards and, with a big smile on his face, say, "Wheee!" And while part of the Karin roller coaster is lots of fun, other parts are not, and for a while Jeff considered leaving me.

Along with the moods came regular thoughts of suicide, which didn't make sense to me because there was nothing in my life that warranted suicidal thoughts. Having the thoughts made me feel even worse about myself because what kind of ungrateful person with my kind of life wants to kill herself? I made one attempt in high school, and it scared me too much to try again. But the thoughts never went away. I don't try to conjure them up; I don't ruminate on them. They are more like visions, impulses. They can come at any time: when I wake up in the morning bracing myself for the day, when I'm standing in the toilet paper section of the grocery store riddled with indecision, during a movie night out with Jeff watching a comedy and listening to everyone else in the theatre laughing. Sometimes they just fly through my head whispering, *take some pills, slice your wrists, jump off the bridge, drive into a tree, no one will miss you, no one will care.* Sometimes they land and stay awhile, festering into a viable option to living.

When I was in my mid-twenties I read a biography about a woman whose name I can't remember now. What I do remember is she had been diagnosed with bipolar disorder, and the description of her symptoms seemed to fit with my erratic mood swings and behaviour. I talked to my family doctor about it and she referred me to a psychiatrist, a frumpy white-haired man in his sixties. At my first appointment, after a brief conversation, he gave me an assessment to fill out with questions like, 'Sometimes I feel extremely over-confident and at other times I feel equally filled with self-doubt' and 'I get into moods where I feel very speeded up and irritable.'

After looking over my answers, he diagnosed me with bipolar 2 rapid cycling disorder. Bipolar 2 consists of depressive episodes alternating with hypomania. Rapid cycling involves having four or more of either type of episode within a twelve-month period. The doctor put me on a prescription of valproic acid, which is used for epileptic patients, but as he explained, "It seems to work for people with bipolar disorder." Because the medication can damage the liver, I needed to have my blood tested regularly and review the results with the psychiatrist. I can't remember how often I went back to see him: once a month or once every few months. What I do remember is how the conversation went.

"Your blood test seems normal. How are you feeling?"

"Fine."

"Good. See you next time."

There may have been a bit more chat than that. Maybe about the weather. But nothing of substance, nothing therapeutic. I don't know whose fault it was. Maybe mine. I believed because I was taking a drug that seems to work for bipolar people that I should be fine. That saying *fine* was the right answer. I didn't know enough about what was going on inside me to know how *fine* should feel. I didn't know how to talk about something about which I knew nothing. I wanted the doctor to feel like he was doing a good job. What I assumed from our interactions was that the drug was the only option to make me feel better, to fix me. He didn't offer any other recommendations. So, I believed that this was purely a brain chemistry problem and the only help was a medication, which *seems to work for some people.*

I continued taking the medication, getting my liver tested and telling the doctor I felt fine, until I became pregnant a year later. Jeff and I weren't planning the pregnancy, but were happy about the news. I went off the medication because it can harm the fetus. At twelve weeks I miscarried. It was mentally and physically painful and we were both disappointed.

I still wanted a child, but I didn't want our child to have an unstable mother. If I was going to be a mom, I was going to have to be normal. I already knew the valproic acid wasn't helping, and I didn't have faith in my indifferent psychiatrist, so I just stopped seeing him and believed I'd have to come up with a plan on my own. And I did. My plan was to act normal, no matter how I felt. And to act normal I had to make rules. And the first rule was to ignore how I feel because how I feel is not an accurate measure of my circumstances.

My friend Mirjana is big on trusting your intuition and inner wisdom. But my intuition regularly says, "Let's end it all. Let's run away to where no one knows us. Let's never leave the house again." It didn't take a psychiatrist to tell me my intuition was broken. So instead of paying attention to my emotions, I made rules and followed them. Rules like, don't kill yourself, get out of bed even though you want to stay in bed all day, don't drink too much caffeine because it makes you spin out of control, don't drink too much alcohol, get enough sleep, exercise, get rid of annoying friends, return phone calls, don't cancel activities and commitments, give yourself a time out if you think you are going to make things worse by talking. I made a lot of rules about not shopping, but I could never follow them. But the other rules seemed easier for me and they worked. They were like pieces to a puzzle of how I think my life should look. And the more correct pieces I have, then the less wrong I am.

But even with all of this structure, with my outward life seeming to be on the right path, I still regularly have suicidal thoughts and become overwhelmed with physical sensations indicating something is wrong and a feeling that something bad will happen if I don't act. The feeling comes first and then I search for what the problem could be. It could be that there is something wrong with the way the furniture is arranged, my wardrobe, the yard, my wardrobe, my hair, my food choices, my wardrobe, my hair, my exercise plan, my wardrobe, my hair, my wardrobe, my social life, my wardrobe, my hair, my hobbies. Every time I think I've solved the problem I have a temporary reprieve from the feeling, but it always returns and the cycle begins again. Most times I return to the same problems: the big winner being my wardrobe and the runner-up my hair. Even though I recognize the cycle is happening, I still cling to the hope that *this* time my fix will work. And as long as I keep to the rules, as long as I stick to the program, as long as I keep finding and fixing problems, then I feel, even if I don't enjoy my life, that I have control of it. I understand it.

But then I go see Val and blab some stupid story about something that happened decades ago and ruin it all.

I'm home from my meeting with Val, home from the mall. I'm lying on my bed with my face pressed into a pillow. I'm not sure why I'm crying. Nothing has changed. Nothing bad happened to me today. It happened a long time ago, and according to the adage, time heals all wounds, I should be over it by now. It should be a non-issue. But another part of me, the one that accepted the pages, knows exactly what is going on. It's like that part of me is a shadowy all-knowing figure in my mind who has been patiently keeping this secret pain from me for over thirty years, knowing I wasn't ready to feel it. But when I told Val the story and she didn't dismiss it, my shadow finally had permission to release it, as if she had taken her finger out of a dam, and when she did, the water didn't trickle in a slow steady stream, it burst the dike open. And now the water is gushing out, threatening to crush me. And while I lie on my bed crying, I argue with myself.

Pay no attention to what Val said. This is ridiculous. I bury my face deeper into my pillow.

Pay attention to how you feel. This is serious, my shadow whispers.

I'm not sure what to do, I don't know who to listen to, but I can't stay in bed and cry all day and there is no way in hell I am looking at those pages Val gave me.

Jeff and I have a weekend getaway planned. We're supposed to leave tomorrow afternoon. I don't want to ruin it for him. I know what to do: ignore the feelings, act normal. I get up off my bed, wash my face, and look at my day planner to see what needs to get done today. I get stuff done.

That night over dinner I tell Jeff about my session with Val. He listens and is compassionate, but I don't think he understands how shook up I am. How can he? I don't understand it either. He offers to cancel the trip, but I can't bear to do that to him.

The next day we head to Manitou Springs Resort. I pray the ninety-minute drive will put distance between me and the gloom that has settled in my chest. I stare out the window and take in the prairie scene: fields of snow-dusted flaxen stubble dotted with aging grain elevators and an occasional deer. Jeff and I chat and listen to the radio. A guitar riff signals a new song and one second into it I recognize it's "Kiss" by Prince. I love this song. I've made an ass out of myself on the dance floor to it more than once. I try to lose myself in the music, let it distract me, generate good-time feelings, but instead, the sexual nature of it is making me feel uncomfortable and I want to turn it off. I tell myself I'm having a ridiculous reaction, it's just a song. But the python around my chest doesn't care what I think and tightens its coil, so I give in and change the station.

We turn off the main highway and drive the few miles to the lake. Jeff navigates down the steep icy hill and pulls up in front of Manitou Springs Resort: a four-storey hotel and spa with an indoor heated pool filled with water pumped in from Little Manitou, the saltwater lake across the street which is advertised as the Dead Sea of Canada. Local legend has it that when smallpox, brought over by European settlers, was decimating Indigenous communities, a small group of Cree men, too sick to move with the rest of their tribe, camped by the lake, took in the healing waters, and recovered. As we carry our bags into the lobby, a spark of hope ignites that maybe a couple of days soaking in the waters will be all I need as well.

After checking in, we have dinner in the hotel restaurant, which overlooks the still, dark lake resting under the cloud-covered sky. I push my chicken alfredo around my plate; the tender noodles steeped in rich creamy sauce aren't comforting me like I hoped they would. After, we soak in the pool and while I think about how lucky I am to be able to have the time and money to afford a weekend getaway, while my arms and legs float effortlessly in the heated, healing waters, something inside me is still falling, still sinking, still pulling me under.

Freshly showered and back at our room, Jeff and I have sex, not because I feel like it, but because that is what is expected when couples have a romantic weekend away. I want things to be normal for Jeff. He shouldn't have to suffer just because I had a bad session with my therapist. He has no way of knowing how I feel. I am a good actor. I've watched enough movies to know how sex should look.

After we are finished, Jeff goes to the bathroom. I lie on my side, staring at the thickly draped windows and a vision pops into my head. It's me in a bathtub with my wrists slit. Despair and confusion flow out with the blood as feelings of warmth, calm and peace envelop me. The image relaxes and soothes me like an oversized thick, fluffy towel just out of the dryer. It's the most inviting impulse I've ever had. I think about the logistics of making it happen, but we only brought safety razors with us and the bathroom is wheelchair accessible and has no tub. Then I get scared. I'm scared that this time I might do it.

When Jeff comes back to bed, he cuddles me for a few minutes and falls asleep. I lie awake, staring at the curtains and considering putting my meeting with Val away in a box and never looking into it again. To go back to the way things were. It wasn't great, but it wasn't what this feeling is now. I was able to avoid this sore spot for most of my life; I should be able to ignore it again. But my shadow sits on my pillow, strokes my hair, and tells me it won't work. Tells me it's too late.

It's the Tuesday after our weekend away, and even though it's almost noon I'm still in bed. I stare at the still-packed bag I took to Manitou sitting listlessly in the corner. The thought of unpacking it, putting things back in drawers, in the bathroom cabinet, in the downstairs laundry, is overwhelming. I'm not ready to face the bag or the day.

Because of my shift-work schedule and the fact that I'd already scheduled days off, I still have four more days off before I have to be back at work. The house is quiet. Jeff is at his job. The kids are at their classes at the nearby university, and I'm alone at home at the bottom of a thirty-year-old pit, feeling the water from the burst dam in my mind pound over me. I roll onto my back and stare at the ceiling. I've already cried once today, when I looked in the mirror after going to the bathroom. I cried over the weekend too. Luckily, I can feel it coming and get to the bathroom before the tears come. I've sobbed through

every shower since my meeting with Val. I'm disappointed at
how weak I am for letting this get to me.

I try to breathe deeply; the python tightens its coil. I give
up. My body aches from being prone, so I get up. I don't know
what to do with myself, so I pace around. Let me rephrase that:
I can't decide what to do with myself. I feel like I have to make a
decision but I can't because I am still arguing with my shadow.

Let's just forget it and go on as usual.

Let's get out those pages and deal with it.

I scowl at the idea of the pages. I won't even look at the
drawer I stashed them in. Instead, I sit at my desk, go online
and search for clothes. I look up new hairstyles. I check out
the makeup sales on my local pharmacy website. I decide I
need a new workout program and scour the internet for ideas.
I go through my closet and try to come up with a minimalist
wardrobe so I can throw the rest of my things out. I look at
flooring options for the kitchen. I look at condos for sale in the
area. I check job postings.

But nothing is helping, because even though I'm stubborn,
I can't deny my crying spells, the heaviness in my chest, and I
know it's not because of my clothes, my hair, my kitchen or my
job. I open the drawer and pull out the pages.

I flip through the pages, get nauseous, throw them back in
the drawer and go back to bed.

3

When I got my first glimpse at Maddie, after she'd been delivered by caesarean section, all I could say was, "she's beautiful, she's so beautiful," over and over until the anesthesiologist put me under because my epidural had worn off while the doctor was still cleaning me out before stitching me up. But before I went under, I heard her crying. The best sound I'd ever heard.

She didn't stop crying for a year.

My friend Tillen tells a story about when his son Peter was a baby and colicky. Once, after being put down for a nap, Peter slept for an unusually long period of time, a time in the house with quiet, no crying. Tillen and his wife, Patsy, became concerned something was wrong with the baby, but they faced a dilemma. If they opened the door, they risked setting off another round of crying, their moment of calm coming to an abrupt end. If they left the door closed, they risked something might be wrong with their baby. Sleep-deprived and with nerves raw from a wailing child, they decided to sit and have a cup of coffee in peace (possibly their last), rationalizing if the baby was fine, there was no sense waking him; if something was wrong, it was probably too late to do anything about it. Either way, I'm pretty sure they didn't enjoy that cup of coffee.

When Tillen tells the story, I understand on a cellular level what he and Patsy felt. One morning, six months into Maddie's year of crying, jangly nerved and exhausted, I opened the fridge to scrounge up breakfast, spotted an old alcoholic cooler abandoned in the back of the fridge and thought, 'This is how it starts. This is why people start drinking.' Now, after my meeting with Val, I begin to understand why people keep drinking.

Over the last three decades I'd only thought a handful of times about what happened to me, but now I can't stop thinking about it. Over and over, I feel the boy grab me from behind. I hear his laugh. I see my classmates and the teacher staring at me. And over and over my body responds with a jolt of adrenaline to my heart, my ribs squeezing the air out of my lungs, my heart trying to beat its way out of its cage. Sometimes the intrusive memories vary from the original event, to the times he held me and invited the other boys in for a feel, to the times he ambushed me in the hallway by my locker in front of friends and anyone else walking by, to the quick little drive-bys that turned into an almost-daily routine. He was like a dog pissing on a tree, marking his territory. Eventually he didn't even need to restrain me because he'd trained the fight out of me, a self-serve grab and grope.

Along with the memories come the whys. Why did I take that class? Why did I keep going back to it? Why didn't I tell anyone? Why didn't I know it mattered until now? Why did it take so long to realize? And along with the whys came the what ifs. What if I'd told someone other than the teacher? What if I'd quit the class? What if I'd fought harder? What if I'd never stopped fighting? What if I'd been smart enough to know what was happening was wrong?

And along with the whys and the what ifs comes a different struggle. A *how could something that didn't physically harm me do so much damage* struggle. A *do I deserve to feel this way* struggle. I rack my brain about how many times it happened. I've always remembered it happening every day. Did it? Maybe shop class wasn't every day. Maybe it was just Monday, Wednesday and Friday. Or maybe just Tuesdays and Thursdays. I try to cast my mind back to the projects we did: a chisel, a tool box, a meat tenderizer. I can't think of any more. We wouldn't have to go every day to finish those projects, would we?

I do calculations in my head. I try to remember how many school days were in a year. I do an internet search. My home state requires schools to be in session for 180 days. Something inside me slumps when I read that number. That's a lot of days to be in class with the boy. Schools are allowed to take six snow days per year, and two days off for hunting season. That would knock off at least eight days which means if class was three times a week it could have happened only one hundred times. If it was two days a week, then only sixty-four times. And, if either of us stayed home sick, if he skipped class, if there were assemblies then it would have happened even less.

I cling to this line of thought and keep going over the numbers, like a reverse auctioneer. Driving the number down with each what if. What if it happened forty times? How about thirty-five, do I hear a thirty-five? Thirty! Twenty-five, I bid twenty-five. Twenty! How low do I need to bid before I don't have to deal with the fallout, with this feeling? Is fifteen times more manageable? How about ten? Can I completely dismiss it at five or less and get on with my life? Why didn't Val ask me how many times? Isn't that important information? While I keep calling out bids, my shadow sits in the back row of the auction, arms crossed with hands jammed into her armpits, shaking her head with her lips pressed in a grim line, murmuring, "It doesn't matter how many times it happened. It's the result that matters. And you know what the result is. You know how you feel."

I concede my shadow has a point, so I pause the auction to see if she has anything else to say. My shadow stands up, points her bidder paddle at me and begins listing off *would yous*. "Would you be thinking this way if it happened to someone else? Would you try to minimize their experience? Would you tell them it was no big deal? Would you tell them they don't have a right to feel bad?"

"Of course not." I slam the gavel down. "Don't be ridiculous."

"How many times would it have to happen to them before you would allow them to feel bad about it?" My shadow makes jabbing motions with the paddle to emphasize her words.

I cross my arms, press my lips together and shake my head. "That's not fair."

"How many times?"

"Once."

"What if this happened to Maddie or Max? How would you feel about it then?" My shadow places her hands on her hips.

"Homicidal."

"So, why can't you feel the same way for yourself?" My shadow stretches her arms out in front of her, palms up.

"Because it's different."

"How?"

"Because the person who did it was a classmate." I bang the gavel on the podium. "He wasn't acting mean." *Bang.* "He didn't call me names or say bad things to me." *Bang.* "He was laughing, and I wasn't hurt and no one did anything, so it couldn't have been a big deal." *Bang.* "It couldn't have been that bad, because I didn't tell anyone, because I never skipped class, because I didn't even try to transfer out of the class." *Bang.* "Because it never seemed to bother me." *Bang.* "Because I don't remember thinking about it before or after class or at all." *Bang.* "Because I didn't even think about the boy, much less hate him or plan my revenge against him." *Bang.* "Because if I thought or did or didn't think or do all of those things, then it didn't matter." *Bang, bang, bang, bang, bang, bang, bang.*

My shadow sighs, considers, then says, "Would you allow any of those excuses if it happened to anyone else? If it happened to Maddie or Max?"

"No."

"Then why do you allow those excuses for yourself?"

"Because it's different for me."

"Why?"

"It just is." My voice quivers and my shoulders fall as I let the gavel drop to the floor.

I still feel like I need to know how many times it happened. I post a message to the high school Facebook group, asking whether anyone remembers how many days a week shop class was.

Seven people reply. Class was five days a week. One hundred eighty days.

I feel sick to my stomach.

Some of the replies include comments about the class and the teacher.

"Great class."

"He was an amazing man."

"He was a blast to work with, we had so much fun in his class…we talk about him all the time."

And one from his daughter, "Dad taught…5 days a week. He always had great stories every year."

Great class, amazing man, a blast to work with, great stories. The comments grate on my nerves, but I can't argue with them. The teacher is a very nice man. He has a very nice family, two boys older than me and a daughter one year younger than me. They went to the same church as my cousins. I worked with them all at the grocery store my dad and uncle owned.

My first job at the store was working in the bottle shed, a small, hot, windowless concrete block building permeated with the acrid tang of stale beer and flat soda pop from all the returnable bottles and cans we sorted by hand. I started there when I was twelve and spent hours working with the teacher's oldest boy. He had a good work ethic and encouraged me to work faster, trying to make a game of the mundane job. He decorated the inside of the building with treasures we found inside the bottles, cans and the bags they came in. Small plastic toys, cheap jewellery, bits and bobs. It was a hot, smelly job in the summer, but I liked working with him. He was kind and respectful. I never heard him say a negative word. After graduating from the bottle shed, I worked with his brother stocking shelves. He, like his brother, coached me into efficiency, or as much efficiency as he could get out of me. I give them both partial credit for my work ethic. Their little sister was a year younger than me and friends with one of my cousins. I didn't know her well, but she was always nice to me when our paths crossed.

So, yeah, the teacher was a good man with strong Christian values who raised great children. I can't argue with any of my former classmates about his character.

But why didn't he stop the boy? Why didn't he help me? I don't think he would have let it happen to his daughter. I think he would have risen to the occasion. So why did he let it happen to me?

Day after day, week after week, month after month.

Maybe it's because he would never have had to intervene for his daughter. Maybe it's because she knew better than to join shop class.

Maybe I should have known better.

When Val started to get through to me, I found myself thinking *the penny is dropping*. Not *the penny dropped*, which implies someone has finally understood or realized something, but *the penny is dropping*, because I was only on the edges of my realization and understanding. And I'm still only on the edges of it. It's like my mind is one of those donation funnels in which a coin spirals around, edging closer and closer to the centre until it finally drops into the vortex in the middle. And I'm scared, because I don't know what's in that vortex. I'm not sure I want to know. What if knowing is worse than how I already feel, than how I've been feeling for the last three decades? But I also don't know how to get out of it, how to stop the penny from swirling, from getting closer to the vortex. And every time it goes around it releases more emotions and pain.

I believe part of the pain is the actual pain I never allowed myself to feel finally being released. Like nine months of being held and groped and gawked at is hitting me all at the same time over and over and over. Another part of the pain feels like grief. When Val suggested the trauma and stress from my *life event* may have been an inciting incident to my subsequent bipolar disorder and the consequences of it, the last three decades flashed through my mind. Decades of shame and regret, suicidal thoughts, hypomania, depression and nervousness and I'm starting to feel a sense of loss for what my life could have been if I'd never taken that class, if the boy had never targeted me, if the teacher had stepped in, if someone would have known how to help me. I feel the loss of how things might have been.

The penny continues to circle for days after my meeting with Val. My mind daily repeats mental gymnastics routines of *what ifs* while waves of pain, intrusive images of the boy grabbing me, and grief over what could have been wash over me. I spend mornings in bed crying and journaling to try to make sense of it. I have to remind myself to shower and eat. I only listen to instrumental music because the sexual nature of most songs makes me grimace. I watch mild shows like *The Golden Girls* and read pleasant books by James Herriott.

Some mornings I wish a gaggle of white-haired grandmas in flowered dresses would sneak into my house and sit in my living room while I cry in my bedroom. I want to hear the soft clicking of their knitting needles and friendly chat muffled by my door. I want to smell the chicken soup they have simmering on the stove. I want them to leave as quietly as they came. I want to open my door to find a freshly knitted afghan, cozy slippers, and tray with soup and oyster crackers. I imagine the great service to society such a group of women could provide. Going house to house, providing presence, leaving gifts of warmth. Instead, I'm stuck with Rosie, Maddie's indifferent brown tabby who whines at my door for her daily ration of wet food and refuses to lie in bed and mope with me.

My friend Norlane is a therapist and I remember her talking about the mental pain associated with PTSD. She said the part of the brain which registers physical pain also registers mental pain, which is why so many people turn to painkillers and alcohol to help them cope, and how the quickest, most effective medicine to shut down the pain associated with PTSD is alcohol. I don't think I am experiencing PTSD, but I am experiencing something. I never drank that cooler back when Maddie was a baby, but I don't have that forbearance now. I white-knuckle it through the day, but by around 4:00 p.m. I'm worn out from the effort and pop a few ibuprofens and wash them down with a glass of wine. I don't want to self-medicate, but I need a respite. I tell myself it's only for a little while; this feeling is bad, but it will pass.

While I argue with myself and wish for grannies, I also start to think about what I am going to do next. Because while I don't fully understand or accept what is happening, I can't deny its effect on me and I feel like I have to do something. I sense that the waves of pain and grief aren't just washing over me, they are also reshaping my shore and leaving behind seaweed, refuse and dead creatures. And even though I believe the waves will eventually subside, I know I will still need to clean up the mess and map out the new coastline. Because I don't think the map I have and the systems I use to keep things cleaned up in my life are going to work anymore. I'm going to have to start over.

I'm going to have to start from scratch.

When I think about starting over, I physically slump as I start to pummel myself with *what ifs*. What if nothing works? What if nothing helps? What if it takes three decades of therapy to get out of this hole? What if it takes more energy than I have? What if it is a waste of time?

"What do you have to lose?" my shadow says softly. And I finally realize she isn't trying to antagonize me. She isn't *questioning* me; she's just asking the question. She doesn't want to deal with this any more than I do. But she knows it has to be dealt with.

What do I have to lose?

I think about the money and days and weeks I've spent shopping online and in the mall. I think about my nervous episodes, my cycle of fixing, my inability to enjoy the blessings in my life, my suicidal thoughts. I think about how much I don't want these things in my life. And I realize just how much I'd like to lose them all.

I get up, go to my dresser, open the drawer, take out the pages, and begin.

4

It's the middle of November: over a week since my session with Val. I stand on the chilly wooden floor of my bedroom and stare at the stack of pages she'd given me. The frosty morning air penetrates the walls. The furnace responds with a groan, then sighs out its warm breath across the floor. Outside my window the howling wind whips snow into swirls under the overcast sky. This will turn out to be the cloudiest November since 1992, the month and year I moved to Saskatoon, but today, Mother Nature gave Saskatoon a silver lining to the winter drear in the form of a thick frosting of rime, turning lifeless bare trees into glistening living sculptures posing in sharp relief against the drab sky. I'm supposed to be at work but instead I called in sick and I'm realizing how lucky I am.

When we call in sick to work, we don't have to explain what we are sick with, but when I call Sergeant Low to let him know I'm not well enough to come to work for the block (two twelve-hour days followed by two twelve-hour nights) I explain why, because I might be out at the library, at the bookstore, on a walk, and someone might see me. I tell Sergeant Low I've had a mental health setback.

Where I come up with these terms, *life event, mental health setback,* I'm not sure. They sound like things that happen to someone else.

Sergeant Low doesn't hesitate to tell me to take all the time I need, not to worry about work, that he understands what it is like. Sergeant Low has been an officer for a while; his last position was in traffic as a collision analyst. When a collision analyst is called to the scene of an accident, it is because someone has been severely injured or, in most cases, died. I've never been to an accident scene where someone has died, where the body or body pieces still lie. I've never even seen a dead body. Sergeant Low has seen a lot of challenging things in his career, a lot of bodies. He openly admits to knowing what it is like to have a mental health setback. I'm lucky he is working when I call.

I know not everyone gets time off when they need it.

I'd recently had a call from a convenience store night shift worker who asked for police to attend because there was a suspicious vehicle in the parking lot. He had been robbed at gunpoint in the store the night before and was nervous it might happen again. While I stayed on the line with him until police arrived, he told me he was shaken up after the robbery, but when he had asked his boss for a night off, his boss had said no.

I wondered if it was his store in which two men fought and one bit the other's ear off. I remember officers coming on the radio saying they were looking for the ear. They never found it.

I wondered if it was his store where another man was stabbed to death. Convenience store workers witness a lot of challenging things too, things too challenging to see for minimum wage with no sick days for a mental health setback. So, while I'm at the lowest point in my life, I know I'm lucky because I have my boss in my corner and time on my side.

I'm very, very lucky.

One of my self-imposed rules to counteract my bipolar moods is: don't write letters. When I am in the midst of a roiling mood, I get seemingly uncontrollable urges to expressively bleed on friends, family and people I barely know through writing letters. At the time, writing them seems like the absolute best idea in the world. But it's usually not. When I write them, they seem like beautiful manifestos of how I am processing a relationship or a thought; when I think about them later, they seem more like incoherent rantings.

But today I give in to the urge and bleed all over my friend and co-worker Jill in an email in which I vomit up every thought that has gone through my head since my meeting with Val. After sending it, instant regret froths in my stomach and I pace the floor between my bed and my desk, mentally flogging myself for not sticking to my rule. I try to tell myself that Jill is my friend. That we've been through a lot together in the last ten years. That between her red fauxhawk and her non-regulation black socks with embroidered skull and crossbones is a loyal and compassionate friend. That revealing the big gaping crack in my sanity isn't going to make her hate me. Telling myself those things doesn't help, so I try to put the email out of my head because now that I've called in sick, I have eight days off to sort myself out before I go back and I'd better get started.

I begin with the pages.

Still in my pyjamas, I sit cross-legged on my bed with a pillow on my lap and my journal and pen beside me. I pick up the pages and begin reading. The introduction explains how people who have been sexually abused often develop coping mechanisms to deal with the resulting trauma.

I frown at the words *sexual abuse* and *trauma* and wonder if Val has given me the wrong pages. I have never considered what happened to me as traumatic or abusive, much less sexually abusive. But to be fair, I never considered what happened as being anything. I think about what the word trauma means, or at least what I think it means. In my mind, trauma is reserved for people who experience significantly disturbing events— rape victims, molested children, physically abused children and partners, soldiers, police officers, victims of war—not for someone pestered by a teenage boy.

I reread the first sentence again. I can't see how the phrase *sexual abuse* applies to me. To me sexual abuse is when someone older molests someone younger: the creepy uncle and his niece, the perverted priest and his altar boy, the degenerate coach and their athlete. Not a classmate with feathered brown hair who laughed and smiled. Besides, there wasn't anything *sexual* about it. The boy didn't get any sexual gratification. At least I don't think he did. I don't remember him rubbing his groin against me. But he must have received some type of gratification, because he always grinned and giggled when he did it. And even though it didn't feel *sexual*, he did touch my sex parts. I don't know what to think, which frustrates me because I like labels, I like certainty, I want to be able to define what happened.

I want to get through these pages and move on with my life, but I can't even get through the first paragraph.

I can't accept that what happened was sexual abuse. So, if it wasn't that, then what was it? How do I define it? I need to look at it from a different perspective. I ask myself, "If a fourteen-year-old called me at the police station and told me the same thing happened to them, what would I call it?" My heart seems to stop and I take a sharp breath.

I know exactly what I'd call it—sexual assault.

I wouldn't hesitate, I wouldn't downplay it or dismiss it. I would tell them that it was one hundred percent, unequivocally, sexual assault. I would do everything in my power to make sure we got a statement from them, so it could be investigated, and I would assure them that the investigating officer would take it seriously and investigate it thoroughly. I know I would tell them this because I have told this to people in similar circumstances. And I know it would be investigated because I've seen it happen.

I once took a call from a woman whose buttocks were groped while on a bus. I didn't roll my eyes when she told me the story. I didn't think she was wasting police time and resources. I didn't think she should just forget about it. I took it seriously, put in a call and the officer assigned to the file pulled the video from the bus and sent it out to everyone in the station in an attempt to identify the suspect. I don't know how it turned out, if the suspect was identified and charged, but I know the officer tried.

Before I became a Special Constable in Communications, I didn't know such an incident constituted sexual assault, and was surprised when my trainer explained it to me. I thought sexual assault only applied to rape. I've been working at the police station, answering calls and questions regarding sexual assault for ten years. How could I have not recognized that what happened to me was sexual assault and why does it still seem like a term that doesn't fit?

It was the early 1980s when I started ninth grade. I wonder what an officer would have said if I told them about what happened. I wonder what the laws were at the time. I think about what the conversation surrounding sexual assault was at the time. I laugh because I know the answer. There was no conversation. There was no *How to Tell if You've Been Sexually Assaulted* quiz in *Teen Magazine*. I think I knew about rape and molestation, but in my mind rape and molestation happened in back alleys and white vans in cities. Rapists and molesters were evil, ugly strangers lurking in the shadows. Stuff like that didn't happen in a small-town school classroom with a nice teacher and surrounded by childhood friends. If I didn't think what happened at the time was wrong, maybe that's why I never viewed what happened as a sexual assault, even after I had learned what sexual assault actually was.

I also begin to wonder if the reason I never thought what happened to me was wrong was because I didn't have the language for it. I remember what I said to the teacher when I begged him to do something, "Please make him stop bothering me."

Bothering me.

That's how I described it. Like he had been playing Keep Away with my pencil case. If the teacher hadn't seen what the boy did and asked me to describe it, what would I have said? I would have been too embarrassed to say breast, butt or genitals. I would have been too embarrassed to point to the places he grabbed. Even if I'd told someone else who hadn't witnessed it, another teacher, my parents, or my older brothers, who might have gone down to the school to teach him a lesson, what could I have said? How could I have described it, if I couldn't bring myself to show or say? What words did I have? Even if I did manage to say he grabbed my breasts, genitals and buttocks, would they have thought it was wrong? A violation? A crime? Would they have helped me? I think about the teacher who repeatedly witnessed it, who saw me struggle to get away. Who I begged for help.

I remember his reaction: a blank look.

Bothering me.

My co-worker Jenn once told me a story about her friend who is a sheriff and works in the courthouse of a small Saskatchewan town. One of this sheriff's duties is guarding during court and she has worked during numerous sexual assault cases. She noticed that when the victims from the town testified, they all used the same term to describe the sexual assault. They called it *a bothering.* It doesn't sound so bad when it's described like that.

I start to accept *logically* that what happened to me was sexual assault, but the term still doesn't feel right, like if I told people I'd been sexually assaulted as a teenager, I would be misleading them. I try a different perspective. A different circumstance. What if a stranger grabbed and groped me in the grocery store, at the mall, in the library? Would I think it was wrong then? Would I consider it sexual assault? A crime? Would I think I had a right to be affected by it?

I look back at the pages. It's a thick stack and I still haven't made it past the first page. I can't fully digest the words *trauma* and *sexual abuse* as applying to me. But Val gave me these sheets for a reason. Maybe, like me, she doesn't think I fully live in the neighbourhood of the sexually abused, maybe she thinks I'm *sexually abused adjacent* and that neighbourhood is close enough. In any case, I decide to trust Val and continue.

The authors talk about how at one point or other everyone uses coping methods to deal with stressful or overwhelming experiences. That ways in which people cope can be helpful, harmful, or both. They explain that coping isn't something to be ashamed of, because when we cope, we are simply doing the best we can to get through a tough situation. They say that recognizing and acknowledging ways in which we cope is one of the first steps in healing and making changes.

I like the idea of healing and making changes so I read on. The introduction is followed by a list of different ways people cope and includes definitions and examples of each. The authors suggest journaling about the ways you've coped and how it has impacted your life. The first example describes how minimizing what happened is a form of coping. My shadow perks up and reads that part again. She raises her eyebrows and gives me a knowing look. I roll my eyes at her, pick up my pen and begin.

I write about minimizing and the next example but not the ones about denying and forgetting because even though I denied it was a meaningful event, I never denied it happened and even though I rarely thought about it, I never forgot it. The examples Val brought up on our session are next and I fill up a few pages in my notebook about them.

There are methods of coping that explain how I can wake up thinking about suicide and then go to work with a smile on my face, how I often feel detached from my body and have a hard time feeling physical pleasure, how I can end a friendship at the drop of a hat.

Some of the examples cover addictions and harmful behaviours. I don't identify with any of the ones mentioned. I'm not sure if my shopping issue is considered an *addiction,* but I include it because it doesn't fall into any other category and I'm pretty sure it's a coping method. I'm not surprised to see my suicide attempt and mental health issues on the list. I spend extra time writing about them.

My born-again Christian phase and sexual history fit neatly into two other categories so I journal about them even though they don't apply to me anymore.

When I finally make it through the pages, I count up the coping methods with which I identified: fifteen.

Fifteen out of twenty-five. Sixty percent. Does checking off fifteen methods mean I've been coping with trauma from sexual abuse? Could there be another reason I checked off fifteen coping methods? Is it possible to identify with fifteen coping methods and not be dealing with trauma, let alone the trauma of sexual abuse? Does Val have some sort of assessment tool somewhere that would tell me what ticking off fifteen coping methods means?

I'm starting to think there is something to why Val took my story so seriously, why she gave me these pages to read. Even though I never thought of what happened as being traumatic, it's getting more difficult to deny the evidence indicating it was.

All of these things, these coping mechanisms, some of them I always thought of not as coping from a *life event*, but as stemming from my defective nature. Some examples I never recognized as being anything other than *that's how life is,* even though I suspected this wasn't how *life was meant to be.* And some examples I never paid attention to, but now that I see them in writing, I realize they are part of how I operate. As it starts to sink in that the cause of many of my problems may be because of what happened to me when I was a teenager, I start to feel relief. Relief because I feel a little less broken, less defective. That maybe the reason I have all these issues isn't because I have a weak character and bad morals. That maybe it is because what happened to me changed me, and reading the pages, I'm beginning to acknowledge that ninth grade and the boy wasn't *just something that happened.*

I check my phone. It's well into the afternoon. Still no reply from Jill. I imagine she is wondering how to make a polite reply as she plots a way to distance herself from me. She's probably already called Human Resources to try to transfer off my shift. Stupid, stupid, stupid. I should have followed my rule.

I drag myself off the bed and look out over the backyard as I stretch my arms and back. The wind has died down. A fat white jackrabbit hops down the path Jeff has shovelled from the deck to the shed. I wonder where it sleeps at night. I head to the kitchen. Make a cup of coffee and some peanut butter toast. Play a half-hearted game of *get-the-string* with Rosie in the living room, then go back to my room, sit at my desk and go online to look up my high school yearbooks. I threw away the physical books years ago because I didn't like high school and I didn't like high school Karin. I've always been hard on past Karin. Mostly high school and college Karin. Why did she spend so much time obsessing about boys? Why couldn't she concentrate on her studies? Why did she waste her natural talents? Why couldn't she maintain friendships? Why couldn't she stop feeling suicidal and appreciate her life? I hear my friends and co-workers talk about their past selves with humour and kindness. I don't have any kindness for past Karin. Just remorse and shame. I don't like to look at pictures of her. I don't like to think about her and I hope to God no one remembers her. I feel like a fact-finding mission can help me piece together what is happening with me. And I think going through the yearbooks will help me figure out when exactly I attempted suicide.

I know it happened in the summer, and I remember it being before I could drive, so it could have been the summer after grade nine. But I also remember it being after Wendy died by suicide. And I thought that happened in the summer after grade ten. But maybe it didn't. I need to know when Wendy died.

I find the yearbooks. I click on 1985.

There I am with my permed hair, feathered bangs and big smile. Oh god, I was so little.

The first day of gym class the teacher weighed and measured us. I was 4'11" and 98 pounds, one of the smallest kids in my grade. But I didn't feel small. I felt larger than life in my cheerleading outfit: white leather tennis shoes, short-sleeved sweater with thick fuzzy felt high school initials sewn on the front, and a short, pleated skirt, all in our school colours: Green and White! Fight! Fight!

In biology I was partnered with a new boy, Mark, who'd moved to town over the summer. He rolled his eyes when I sat next to him.

"Oh, great, my partner's a dumb cheerleader," he scoffed.

I smiled. It didn't bother me. I knew I was smart. I'd show him. And I did. A few weeks later I got perfect marks on our first test; he didn't. He admitted he was impressed and we became friends. But then my grades started to drop. For some reason it became harder to concentrate. It's starting to dawn on me now why that might have been.

I keep scrolling through the pages. There's Wendy. She's a pretty brunette with soft brown eyes and a gentle smile. She lived a few doors down from me. When we were younger we played together in the summers but hung out with different friends in school.

We stayed friendly though. We took the same bus to school and usually walked to and from the bus stop together, chatting on our way. One day as we were walking, Wendy told me a secret. Something that had happened to her when she was younger. Something that now, as an adult, I understand falls squarely under the category of *children needing to see a therapist*. When she told me, I was shocked into silence. Nothing in my experience or knowledge of the world had prepared me for this kind of information. I had no idea what to say to her and I didn't ask any questions. I never told anyone what she revealed to me, but I wish I had. I often wonder if I'd told someone if it would have made a difference. If Wendy would have gotten the help she needed.

I keep scrolling.

There's the boy with his feathered brown hair and charming smile.

Just looking at his picture makes my stomach contract, pushing bile into my throat.

There's the teacher. He looks younger than I remember. He was probably around the age I am now. He looks kind and friendly. I don't remember thinking at the time that he was handsome, but he was. I remember that all of his students loved his class. Told fun stories about him. Because he was a good guy. One of the good ones.

I scroll through more pages. A photo of my ninth-grade algebra teacher reminds me of the day I had a laughing fit in his class. I don't remember now what set me off, but I started to laugh, quietly at first, then louder and more hysterically. I tried to hold it in, but the laughter was too strong. It felt like I'd explode if I didn't let it out. People close to me noticed first. I couldn't stop. I shrieked with laughter, tears streamed down my face, one hand held my aching stomach, the other clutched my chair so I wouldn't fall off. The class stopped, everyone stared at me. I remember staring at me too, from outside my body. I looked like a crazy person.

I don't find what I'm looking for in 1985, so I click on 1986. I start at the back of the book in the ads. I remember Wendy's friends paid for a memorial ad because the school didn't acknowledge her death. It's not there. I scroll through the rest of the pages, starting from the beginning.

I'd quit the cheerleading squad by then, although I don't remember why. I didn't really care about the purpose of cheerleading, but I loved the routines, the dancing, the joking around and spending time with my girlfriends. And I loved the uniform. God, how I loved that uniform. Why would I quit something I enjoyed so much?

There I am in my tiara and fake fur coat: I am the homecoming class representative. I am sitting between the eleventh- and ninth-grade representatives on the back of a truck driving around the football field at the homecoming game. Somewhere in my mother's photo albums is a picture of me with my date. I don't remember his name or where he came from. I remember he is from the beginning of my collection of boys. Boys I had to have, but didn't want to keep.

I keep paging through, but still don't see any photos of Wendy. I come across a full-page article about a senior who died in an accident and a scholarship his parents set up for his classmates, but there is no mention of Wendy's death. Finally, many pages later, there's Wendy. She has bangs in this photo. It softens her face even more.

I click on 1987. Go through the front pages. No Wendy. I go through the sports section. No Wendy. Go through the class photos. No Wendy. Wendy isn't there. I scroll through the rest of the pages. There's me laughing and dancing in the gym in front of the class assembly. There I am doing improv in drama class. There's me looking at a map alongside an article about me going to Australia as an exchange student.

I remember begging my parents to go on the exchange program. Our family had hosted two exchange students when I was younger, but I'd never thought of being one. Not until 1986. All of a sudden, I had to go somewhere. I didn't care where. Dad said only if I could pay for it. I racked my brain. "What about the money Nana gave me?" Dad relented. I left the winter of 1987 for a year.

When I came back, one of my friends asked, "How could you just leave like that?"

I didn't know how to answer. Didn't everyone want to leave?

I click on 1988. This time I start at the beginning. There's me in the school beauty pageant. Big permed hair, sparkly dress with a hooped skirt, matching elbow-length fingerless gloves. I keep looking for some kind of memorial page for Wendy. Then I finally find it. It's on the last page after all the other ads. A half-page ad paid for by her friends. There's a photo of Wendy with her short brunette hair, deep brown eyes, and pretty smile. Kind words from a friend printed on one side, a poem Wendy wrote on the other. The poem is about biology. I remember how Wendy loved science and nature. One day at the bus stop she showed me a treasure. A skinned preserved cat in a clear plastic bag. She was so proud to have something so interesting to show her classmates at school. I don't remember if the teacher allowed her to show it in class.

May 1970–June 1986

So that's when she died. Huh. I'd thought it was earlier. It seems strange that there was no mention of it until the 1988 yearbook, but I guess her friends had stepped up when the school didn't.

I'd heard her death was deemed a suicide by firearm.

When I heard about Wendy's suicide, I didn't feel anything. People said they didn't understand how someone could do that. But I remember understanding, just not with words.

My mom took me to the funeral. We sat in the back. The minister droned on about all of the things Wendy would have wanted. I was furious. If everyone knew what Wendy wanted, then how come she died?

1986. I look at the yearbook again. I thought my attempt was earlier. But it was definitely after Wendy died, and it wasn't after I came back from Australia. So, it must have been later that same summer. I have a vague recollection that it was a Saturday morning in late August. But I can't be sure.

I remember that I wanted to do something with a boy that day. A boy I had to have. Mom said no. But I wanted what I wanted so I argued. Her answer stayed the same. She went outside to work in her garden. I ran upstairs. Past my bedroom with the pretty flowered yellow wallpaper and white ruffled curtains. Past my dad's shiny oak rifle case with the key in the lock, past my mom's sewing machine, into my brothers' old bedroom.

I opened the closet where I knew the gun was kept, and took out the box. It was small but heavy. I opened it. I stared at the gun. It looked funny to me. Maybe it wasn't even a real gun. But the bullets looked real. I didn't know how to use a handgun, but loading it was easy. I cocked the gun and held it to my temple. I don't think I really wanted to die. But the feeling was too strong. Like the day in algebra class, when I was so overwhelmed with feeling that I couldn't control myself.

But this time the overwhelming feeling didn't make me laugh. It felt like I was filled with locusts exponentially multiplying inside me, the pressure of their wings beating hysterically around my body, their jaws eating up my insides. Getting a boy helped me relieve the pressure. But I couldn't get one that day.

I changed the angle of the gun so the barrel was at a forty-five-degree angle, thinking maybe if I just blew a quarter of my head off, I'd get relief. I closed my eyes and pulled the trigger. It stopped halfway. I couldn't get it to move any farther. I held the gun in front of me, trying to figure out what was wrong. I couldn't find a safety; I couldn't find anything. I pulled and pulled. The trigger wouldn't budge.

I started to cry, then sob, chest heaving, eyes streaming, snot running, gun in my lap. I remember seeing myself from above. I remember thinking I looked like a crazy person. I remember being repulsed at what I saw.

My parents never knew I'd tried to shoot myself. Every now and then I get a 911 call at work about a teenager or child who suicides after a routine argument with a parent. There is no note, no warning signs. After the call I want to contact the parent and let them know it is not their fault. Kids are good at looking normal, acting fine, they don't know how to express what is going on inside of them because they don't understand what is going on inside of them. If my mom had walked into the room and seen me with the gun in my lap, I think I know how the conversation would have gone: *What are you doing? Are you okay? Nothing, I'm fine.* It wasn't her fault.

Now I'm starting to think it wasn't my fault either.

Now, as I look at past Karin, I don't cringe when I see her. I'm starting to see her in a new light, through a new lens. I see her for who she really was. Just a child. A fourteen-year-old child who was repeatedly humiliated in front of her classmates and teacher. And I feel sad for her. I feel angry for her. I feel homicidal for her, like she is my own child. I wish I could go back and fight for her because she deserved better than that. She deserved to be able to go to school and feel safe. She deserved to try new things like metal shop and not be punished. She deserved to be listened to and helped by her teacher.

I'm also starting to understand why she did the things she did. Why she had serial sexual relationships. Why her moods were out of whack. Why she couldn't maintain friendships. Why she couldn't stay out of the damn clothes store. Why she became obsessed with being a born-again Christian and threw out all of her and her husband's CDs that didn't glorify God. Why she became obsessed with being a minimalist and threw out almost all of the rest of their stuff. Why she became obsessed with every new lifestyle craze. Why the suicidal thoughts never let her be. And I see that all of this isn't because she was weak or stupid or irresponsible. I see that she sensed that somewhere there was a really big problem that needed to be fixed, and she just couldn't see it, but she could feel it, all the time, everywhere. So instead she looked for what the problem could be. Maybe it's this, maybe it's that, She'd latch onto something and try to fix and fix and fix it. And it seemed to work for a brief period of time, but then that feeling came back in another wave, which meant there must be something else wrong in her life. Something else that needed to be fixed, and she did it all over again. And it's not her fault, because she didn't know. Maybe she wasn't ready to know.

But now I do. And I can look back at all the things I've been ashamed of and see that what was really happening was that I was coping. I was protecting myself the best I could. And this is huge, this compassion I feel for past Karin. I hope it stays and I hope that someday I will be able to feel that way for right now Karin.

I hear faint scratching and look over to see one of Rosie's eyes peering at me through the narrow gap of the almost closed door. I stare back at her and wait to see if she'll try to push the door open to let herself in. She lets out a plaintive *mew*. I can't tell if her door-opening neurons aren't firing, if she's lazy, or she just likes to make me do things for her. Still, I get up, let her in and arrange the duvet on my bed to her liking. She jumps up into the spot I've fixed for her, kneads the bedding with her paws and lies down. I sit down next to her, give her a scratch behind her ears and look at my coping list again. I don't use all of the ways of coping all the time, and some of them I don't use anymore. The ones I do use vary on the scale of intensity and frequency.

The pages end with the exhortation to forgive yourself for the coping mechanisms you have used to survive. The authors encourage you to leave the feeling of shame behind. To love and accept yourself and recognize that you are no longer a helpless child, but an adult with agency.

I put the pages and journal down and lie back in bed, check my phone and cringe when I see Jill has replied. I squint my eyes as I open it up, not wanting to see all the horror of her response at one time. But instead of gore, I find phrases such as "Thank you for trusting me …it wasn't your fault….I'm so sorry what you went through…it breaks my heart…I believe in you…" and my favourite, "I would have gotten expelled from school for beating the shit out of that boy."

I reread the email a few times and even though I'm still wallowing in the pit, I know I'm lucky. I'm very, very lucky.

It's been a few days since I've finished going through Val's pages. I'm still getting intrusive thoughts of the boy grabbing me. With every thought comes the tight grip of the python, a resurgence of the locusts, my heart trying to beat its way out of my body, all of it leaving my chest sore and heavy, my forehead throbbing. I haven't showered or eaten yet today. Rivers of tears course under my skin threatening to overwhelm me at any given moment. I'm still taking regular doses of ibuprofen throughout the day and drinking wine at night.

But something is shifting, opening.

Light is beginning to seep through. Maybe having compassion for past Karin is the beginning of change. Maybe if that can change, other things can change as well. I start to think that what happened to me was like an earthquake in the middle of the ocean and part of me knew the tsunami was coming and tried to protect me by building a hut of twigs and seaweed on the beach. My coping hut. But now I see the hut for what it really is and know it's not going to stand up to the waves any longer and I can't stay on this beach anymore. It's time to get to higher ground. But to do so I'm going to need a map, some directions, a guide. It's three weeks until my next meeting with Val. I can't wait that long so I have a shower, eat something, and head to the bookstore.

Inside the store I'm assaulted by holiday tunes and displays reminding me to be merry and full of joy. I consider writing my city councillor to request seasonal songs and decorations be limited to the month in which the holiday occurs. I wander around the maze of bookshelves because there is no way in hell I'm going to ask someone where the trauma section is. I finally find it in the self-help section on the bottom shelf: a sadly small collection that doesn't even take up half of the shelf in a bookstore that has a whole section dedicated to adult colouring books.

I break into a cold sweat and tremble as I read the titles. "This reaction is ridiculous," I think, then feel my unbidden physical responses to stress rear their ugly heads. *Twitch, ribbit, stretch*. I look around to make sure no one has seen me. I find the book I'm looking for: *The Courage to Heal*. When Val gave me the pages, she cautioned I might not want to get it in case it is triggering, but I want to see for myself. I pull the book out and try to rifle through it, but my shaking hands aren't cooperating and I can't make my eyes focus on the words.

"It's only a book." *Twitch, ribbit, stretch*. But telling myself that doesn't work. I put it back. And have a look through the books near it. None of them interest me. I conclude that going home and doing an online search might be better. *Twitch, ribbit, stretch*. But first I'll go to the mall across the parking lot and do some clothes shopping.

5

Jeff and I hadn't been married long when I woke him up in the middle of the night and asked him if I had killed anyone. We also hadn't known each other long. We'd first met the summer after I graduated from university. I worked on campus in a graduate dorm cafeteria which housed summer students and people attending seminars. Jeff was there participating in a six-week science fiction and fantasy writing workshop. He had beautiful wavy blond hair and wore tank tops that showed off his chiselled shoulders, but it was his playful banter that made me notice him. The first week he nicknamed me "Sunshine" because I seemed so bright and cheery. The second week he sang "You Are My Sunshine" to me while I rang up his order. We dated the remaining four weeks and he stayed an extra week to make it five. He went back to Saskatchewan in August and came back for a week in September. I moved to Canada in November and we were married in January. We married so quickly that at the wedding reception my brother Steve asked, "How far along are you?"

"I'm not pregnant." I scowled back.

"No, really, you can tell me," he prodded. I rolled my eyes and walked away.

We got married so quickly that after the wedding, my dad pulled Jeff aside and said, "Give her a year. If it doesn't work out you can send her back."

We got married so quickly, our brother-in-law Bernie gave the marriage six months. On our anniversary we always make a toast to Bernie.

So, after less than a year together, when I woke Jeff up to ask him if I had killed anyone, his response of shrinking back into his pillow, pulling the covers up to his nose, and squeaking, "I don't know," was reasonable.

I woke him up because I'd dreamt the police knew I'd killed someone and were on their way to arrest me and dig up the body. The body I'd buried. The body with its head cut off. The dream was so vivid that when I woke from it, I wasn't sure if it was real, which is why I woke up Jeff. But he wasn't any help, so I had to think it through myself. I didn't remember killing anyone, but I'd heard people have killed during bouts of temporary insanity and not remembered, so maybe I did. But how long does a bout of temporary insanity last? Surely not long enough to cut off a head. I struggle at disjointing a chicken, and I'm sure cutting off a human head must be much harder. I'd for sure remember that. And what about digging a grave? That is a lot of work. Temporary insanity couldn't last as long as it would take for me to dig a hole and bury a body. As I reasoned, I began to realize it was just a dream and started to calm down. I turned to Jeff and said, "I don't think I killed anyone." Then I lay down and went to sleep. I don't know how well Jeff slept that night.

The *body in the backyard* is one of a triad of recurring dreams I've been having since my teens. In the first dream, someone's chasing me, hunting me, catching me, holding me. Beating me, choking me, stabbing me, drowning me. My legs try to run, but I can't feel them. My arms try to fight, but they're not there. My mouth opens to scream, but my throat is empty. I'm not in a room. I'm not outdoors. I'm not in a place. I'm surrounded by emptiness, falling into darkness. And I'm alone. Other than my attacker, I'm always alone.

Petrified and alone.

In the second dream I chase, I catch, I hold, I fall down and bring them down with me. I punch, I beat, I choke, I stab. I survive by slaying. There's no in between. It's me or them. I'm murderous. A murderess. There is no backdrop, no context, no story, no scene, just struggle and fight. And still, I'm alone. Other than my attacker, I'm always alone.

Terrified and alone.

In the third dream, the police are coming because they know about the body buried in the backyard. The body with its head cut off, that I cut off. I have to get rid of it. But it's daylight. If I dig it up, someone will see. If I dig it up, it will be too heavy for me to carry. It will fall apart from decay, body pieces everywhere. I won't be able to handle it all. I won't be able to hide it all. And I'm alone, I'm always alone.

Horrified and alone.

I wake up from all three dreams paralyzed with fear, my heart racing, my body drenched in sweat. It takes me many minutes before I can move, before I can fully realize what's real and what isn't. In the *body in the backyard* dream, I am always in my childhood bedroom when I learn the police are coming. For years as a teenager, after waking from that dream, I would stare wide-eyed at the ceiling, afraid to get out of bed and look out the window for fear of seeing my parents' yard littered with graves. When I would finally screw up the courage to look out the window and see that nothing was there, I would wonder if instead of burying the bodies in the lawn, I'd been burying them in the woods beyond the yard where they would be harder to find.

I've been thinking about these dreams because lately I've been reading some books about the effects of trauma, one of which is Dr. Peter A. Levine's *Waking the Tiger: Healing Trauma*. I'd seen the book online and one line in the description resonated with me: "*People are often traumatized by seemingly ordinary experiences*." After my failed bookstore foray, I ordered it and a few other books online and stayed close to my front door until they arrived two days later.

Reading the books in the comfy confines of my room, sitting up against a berm of pillows, a puffy duvet cocooning my legs while warm air blows out of the heating vent to chase away the mid-November chill, I find myself nodding along as

I read, saying, Yes! Yes! as the writers give language to describe what I've felt has been happening within me for the last three decades. Relief washes over me as they sort out the enigma that is trauma and explain it in a way that helps me make sense of how what happened to me could have affected me so strongly.

I read about the three involuntary reactions to danger. All three reactions begin in the amygdala, the part of our brain that perceives threat. When the amygdala senses danger it alerts the hypothalamus, which activates the autonomic nervous system (ANS). The ANS then triggers natural responses that create hormonal and physiological changes in the body. These changes result in flight, fight or freeze.

Apparently, the amygdala isn't very discerning. If it perceives threat, whether objectively life-threatening or not, it puts the body on high alert. I'm reminded of the viral online videos in which people put cucumbers on the ground behind their cat while it is eating. When the cat turns around, it freaks out and leaps out of the way, thinking the cucumber is a deadly threat instead of a bland vegetable. The ANS serves a very useful purpose, because in that split second, the cat doesn't have time to determine the level of threat, so it takes the safe route by fleeing. After the cat is safely out of the way of the innocuous green gourd, and realizes it's not a predator, the cat's nervous system reregulates, becomes curious, and the cat moves towards the cucumber to investigate.

According to Dr. Levine, threatening experiences can manifest symptoms of trauma when a person's body is unable to reregulate naturally. Instead of moving through the natural process of reregulation, a person becomes stuck in the experience. To me it sounds like malware on a computer. The threatening experience doesn't just appear on the screen, it infects the whole operating system, causing a chain reaction of problems or symptoms in how it operates. Like malware on a computer, if symptoms of trauma aren't recognized and treated, they may persist and worsen, which in turn can adversely affect a person's quality of life.

Before reading the books, I was familiar with the fight-or-flight response, but I'd never thought much about the freeze response. When I first joined the police service, I regularly worked out at the station gym on my lunch break. Because I was new, patrol officers, who were also working out, introduced themselves. A few of them, upon learning I worked as a special constable in communications, asked if I had plans to apply to become a regular constable. They asked this because they couldn't comprehend why anyone in their right mind would choose to be cooped up answering the phone for twelve hours. I'd never considered being a regular constable, even though when I had taken the entrance exam, I had been in a room full of people applying to become regulars; even though I had been sworn in alongside another woman my age who was hired as a regular.

The first time an officer asked me, it planted the idea in my head. An idea I thought about for approximately five minutes before completely dismissing it. I dismissed it because when I watch police shows on TV, fact or fiction, and see officers approaching danger, I always think *I could never do that*. Not because I wouldn't like to save the hostage from the armed gunman, be the hero, but because I knew I could never physically make my body move in that situation. Now that I'm learning that traumatic symptoms can be a result of perceived threat, I'm starting to think it had something to do with what happened in ninth grade. Maybe because fighting wasn't effective and fleeing didn't seem to be an option, my body switched gears into freeze, and let the boy grope me every single time. If that happened regularly for nine months, maybe that was enough to have damaged me. It also helps to learn that my problems may have stemmed from an instinctual response, a response over which I have no control. It helps me feel less embarrassed for not being strong enough to weather ninth grade unscathed.

As I'm reading about the fight, flight and freeze responses and thinking about my dreams, I start to see a connection. Dream number one seems to be my freeze response and dream number two my fight response. I'm not sure what dream number three is about, but it doesn't seem to be the flee response. I wonder why I don't have a flee response dream and then I remember another recurring dream I've never connected with the others. It's a dream in which I am desperately running away from high school, trying to get home. But instead of getting closer to home, I keep finding myself passing the same landmarks, back at the front door of the school, running up the same hill and I can never seem to make it home. I have the same feeling of panic, frustration and fear as I do in the other three dreams. Maybe that is my flee response.

I've never given much thought to the dreams because I've always had scary dreams, dreams so frightening that on waking from them in the middle of the night, I'd often go sleep on the floor of my siblings' rooms or outside the door of my parents' bedroom, and for years, I was afraid to go to sleep. But the scary dreams when I was little are markedly different than the ones that started when I was a teenager and I'm starting to think they might be connected with what happened in ninth grade. I know that nightmares are a symptom of trauma, particularly Post Traumatic Stress Disorder, but I always assumed it meant the nightmares had to be a reliving of the actual event. Maybe that's not the case. Maybe my fight, flight and freeze dreams are an attempt by my subconscious mind to deal with the unresolved trauma of ninth grade.

I start to wonder, if my dreams are a symptom of trauma, then maybe I have PTSD. I wonder this because I know that some people diagnosed with PTSD are eligible for service dogs. I've often talked about how nice it would be to have a dog I could take to work with me, to have it lay its big warm head on my lap while I take a call from someone who tells me he hopes god reserves a special place in hell for me after I've advised him to call the SPCA and not 911 for an abandoned kitten. Or a female so hopped-up on meth she is punching holes in her walls with a hammer because she believes people are hiding in them. Or a mother who has woken up to find her baby died in its sleep. After calls like those it would be nice to run my fingers through the dog's soft, warm fur. Feel the gentle rise and fall of its chest. Stare into its non-judgemental eyes. I bet all of those callers could use a service dog too.

I go online and look up the symptoms of PTSD. I check off a lot of boxes, but don't know if that means I would be diagnosed with it. I search online to see if I would qualify for a dog. A dog that will calm me, make me feel safe, take away my bad dreams and suicidal thoughts, keep me out of the mall. I find numerous sites with pictures of smiling people and their furry friends. I want to be one of those people; I want to have that furry friend. I read about what kind of mental health issue warrants having a service dog—a mental health issue which prevents me from performing at least one necessary life task without help daily. That's not me. I'm a little disappointed.

As if on cue to my brief disappointment at not being mentally ill enough to get a service dog, Rosie saunters into the room and stares at me impassively. She jumps on my desk to play with a pen I'm fiddling with, then looks at me, then at the computer monitor, then at me again. I give her head a scratch and put on a YouTube video of chipmunks for her. If I'm stuck with Rosie and can't have a dog to solve my problems, I guess I'm going to have to try something else.

According to the pages Val gave me, disconnecting the mind from the body is something a person unconsciously does to cope with the barrage of overwhelming physical sensations a traumatized body can experience. One way to begin to heal trauma is to reconnect the mind with the body. To reteach the mind that the body is a safe place.

Mind and body disconnect. I think of how, at the slightest provocation, my mind checks out and my body goes on autopilot. Reconnecting the mind and body sounds a little new age-y to me but I decide to give it a try anyway. I do an internet search about how to reconnect the mind to the body and find one suggested method is a body scan meditation. I search for a body scan video, queue it up, pop in my earphones and begin.

The video starts with the sound of soothing ocean waves, which alerts my bladder that I need to pee.

I go pee, come back, put in the earphones and start at the beginning. After thirty seconds of waves, a gentle baritone voice makes an entrance and instructs me to lie down in a comfortable position.

I pause the recording, remove all the extra pillows, books, and journals that are crowding my bed and lie down. I hit play and listen to more waves. The baritone voice returns and invites me to take four deep breaths.

I consider the challenge but then decide to let the sleeping python around my ribcage lie and wait until the narrator finishes showing off his deep-breathing abilities while I sip breath into my lungs. Once the baritone has reached optimum relaxation from his four magical deep breaths, he guides me to focus on my body one part at a time, starting at my forehead.

I think about my forehead. I try to feel my forehead. The skin, the muscles underneath the skin, my skull. I send all my attention to the space between my eyebrows and my hairline. I will myself to be present in this small patch of skin on my body. I fail. I decide to cheat and gently massage my forehead with my fingers.

I know that my fingers are there. I can sense them on my forehead. But I don't really *feel* them. It's like when I had an epidural when I gave birth to Max. I could feel the pressure of what was happening, but not the sensation of it. I'm not completely numb. I feel temperature and pain and I'm ticklish, but other touch, touch that should feel pleasurable, doesn't register with me. Other than close family, I can't wait for hugs to end. I endure massages. The meaning of the word *caress* is completely lost on me. The voice encourages me to stay in my forehead, feel the subtle changes of sensation in my forehead. I squeeze my eyes, try to envision my forehead and will it to feel. Still nothing.

I continue on with the exercise until the voice runs out of body parts. I can't tell if it's having any effect, but at least

I've had a little rest, a bit of relief from the weight I've been experiencing.

I repeat the exercise on the following days and try some of the other ones I've read about. They seem too simple to heal something as dooming as the word *trauma* suggests. I picture the act of healing trauma as having to be as big and dramatic as the original event. Like in movies when an anvil falls on someone's head and they get amnesia. The only way they get their memories back is by having another anvil fall on their head. But the exercises I try are gentle, subtle, and my mood improves a little every day. I don't know if it is time that is making the difference or the exercises. Either way it feels good to be doing something.

It's been two weeks since I last saw Val. I'm no longer crying every day, but I'm starting to get worn down by sudden flashbacks of the boy sneaking up behind me, seizing me in his arms, his hands taking turns gripping my crotch, grabbing at my breasts, groping my butt. At the same time, shockwaves of electricity burst in my heart, the vice-like grip of the python squeezes the air out of my lungs, and the locusts erupt into a violent flurry, while a wave of nausea and shame washes over me as I feel the eyes of my classmates and the teacher watching the boy violate me. I tell myself to stop thinking about it.

Telling myself doesn't work.

In *Waking the Tiger*, Dr. Levine describes how he guided two of his clients through an exercise in which they experienced the physical symptoms of trauma, either with the memory of the event or independent of the memory and helped them move through the freeze response into action. He instructed one woman, who was experiencing symptoms of panic, to visualize tigers were after her, and to imagine herself running to a tree and climbing it. Levine guided another client through a traumatic memory with prompts to ground the man in a comforting memory and to move his arms and legs to mimic the fight and flight response. The idea isn't to relive the moment as it actually occurred, but to renegotiate it. Tired of the barrage of images of the boy and his hands, having gone to a therapist a total of four times, read a bit about trauma, and not really understanding what renegotiating trauma means or how it should be done, I decide I'm qualified enough to try it on my own.

Even though no one is home, I lock the door to my bedroom. I lie down on my bed. I close my eyes and imagine my first day of high school. It's the first week of September and our small resort town already feels quieter now that the summer tourists have gone back to their cities. I'm in my cheerleading uniform but have sweatpants on under the skirt for the bus ride to school because the mornings are cool. As soon as we arrive at school, I take off my sweatpants and shove them in my locker. I walk down the long hallway to the metal shop class. It's a large, high-ceilinged, concrete block room filled with bulky unfamiliar machinery. The air smells tinny. Class begins and I stand with my classmates, some of whom I've known and been friends with since kindergarten, listening to the teacher give a talk on what we can expect for the next year. The boy comes up from behind and grabs me. But this time I'm stronger than he is, and I throw his arms off of me, turn around and pummel him.

I open my eyes and shake my head to erase the image. I don't feel good about beating him up.

I close my eyes again. I'm back in class, listening to the teacher, when the boy grabs me from behind.

I open my eyes and shake my head again. I tell myself that this is *my* story and I don't have to let the boy grab me at all. I start over.

I picture myself in class. I'm wearing my cheerleading uniform, but this time I'm also wearing a cape. The boy comes at me from behind, but this time I hear his creepy little footsteps with my bionic hearing and before he can seize me, restrain me, laugh in my ear, grope my breasts, grab my crotch, before all the other boys and the teacher just watch and do nothing to stop him: I whirl around, cape slicing through the air, brace my legs one in front of the other, push against his chest with both hands and with my supersonic voice yell, "NO!"

Animated rings spring from my mouth. The boy, the teacher, and the rest of the class are blown back against the wall by my powerful shout. I turn and run to the door, fling it open, run down the hallway, through the main entrance and out to the road. I turn and run down the main road past the beach and the Dairy Queen. I turn at the intersection and race past the grocery store, the playground and the trailer park. I slow down near the road leading to my house. I want to turn there. I want to feel safe there. I want it to be far enough. But the space between my heart and my throat says, "Not yet." "Sorry, Mom and Dad," I say and keep running. I look down, I'm wearing super-hero boots, I can run as far as I need to. I run all the way through my state. Westward ho! I race through cities and farmland, then turn north, hop across rivers and jump over lakes until I leap the border into Saskatchewan and race into Saskatoon into the arms of Jeff, Maddie and Max. They wrap their arms around me and keep their eyes on the horizon while I catch my breath and Rosie weaves herself between our legs. Leaning against my family, surrounded and safe, I look back at from where I came. All I see is wide open prairie.

I open my eyes. I feel spent, like I *have* fought and fled. I'm not sure if I did it right, but I feel a little better. I wonder if, for it to work, I need to do it for every time it happened. Over the next few days whenever the image of the boy comes to me, whenever I feel him coming up from behind, I fight. Sometimes I push him and run away before he gets me. But sometimes he gets me first so I throw him off, spin around and pound him with my fists until he disappears.

I'm the youngest of four children. My oldest brother, Dave, is nine years older than me, Steve is seven years older and my sister is five years older. I have amiable relationships with all of them, but because of the age difference I've never been particularly close with them. Still, I've been wanting to tell someone from my family about what's been going on with me. But not my parents. I don't like to trouble them with my troubles. I talk with Dave three times a year: his birthday, my birthday and on my yearly visit home. My sister has too much going on in her own life and doesn't need to hear about my *issues*. Steve is the one I talk with the most so, when he calls me the next day, he is the big winner in Karin's personal story revelation roulette.

With a shaky voice, I tell Steve about what happened to me in ninth grade, my obliviousness of how it affected me, my meeting with Val and the fallout. I tell him how I'm having a hard time, struggling.

"I'm surprised that happened to you."

"Yeah? Why?"

"Well, I can't believe that the teacher let that happen. I've always considered him to be a very moral man."

A very moral man.

I know why my brother says this. Because the teacher isn't just a teacher. He's a man we know. Our family knows. A friendly acquaintance. A man known as a church-going man. An upright man. A man who raised very nice and respectful sons I know and worked with at my summer job.

A very moral man.

"Yeah, I know," I say, wondering if my brother believes me. Wondering if my testimony holds up against the reputation of *a very moral man*. But then Steve asks who the boy is, and I tell him.

"Do you want me to take care of him?"

Take care of him? What would that even look like? A stern talking to? A beating behind a bar? A hunting accident?

"Thanks, but I don't feel like I need revenge. I don't think it would make me feel any better." What I don't say is that I'm *taking care of him* regularly when I'm assaulted by visions of him.

Two nights after I first lay down and attempted to renegotiate my trauma, I have the *body in the backyard* dream. But this time it's not the backyard of my parents' house. It's my backyard. I need to bury a big bag of garbage. I dig a hole by the shed. But it isn't a hole, it's a grave in which I've already buried a body in a green garbage bag. I don't know who is in the bag or how they died. But I know I had something to do with their death, and I buried them there. It doesn't look big, it's not a little kid, but not an adult either. At first the grave seems shallow, but then it becomes deeper and filled with all sorts of rubbish: electronics, old toys, shoes and soon the whole corner of the yard is filled with junk. It's too much for me to handle, I don't know what to do. I don't know where to begin. I start to panic.

Then Jeff appears by my side. He takes my hand and says, "We'll bury this bag of garbage in with the body to cover the smell, and take the rest of the stuff to the dump."

Then he bends down and picks up an old radio, a Fisher-Price popper push toy and an old boot.

I wake up, and for the first time after *the body in the backyard* dream I don't feel afraid. I don't feel alone. I lie awake, staring at the ceiling, feeling this new feeling devoid of racing heart and I feel something new. I feel my chest expanding wider than usual, my stomach rising and falling without effort and I think, "This must be what it feels like to take a real breath."

I breathe deeper to test the edges, find out how far I can go before I feel the python tighten around my ribs. But I never reach that point; the python is gone and I think, "Holy shit, it worked!"

6

'm fascinated by scams. I've watched multiple documentaries and listened to a six-part podcast on Bernie Madoff alone. I'm astounded by both the audacity of scammers and the naivety of the scammed. It's almost unbelievable the number of calls I receive at work from people who have just spent hundreds of dollars on gift cards to keep from being arrested by the Canada Revenue Agency. And that's just one of the many current scams. I remember, years ago, a couple invited Jeff and me to a dinner where we could learn about an incredible real estate investment opportunity, with a guaranteed return of at least twenty percent but possibly up to sixty percent. When I suggested to the wife the investment sounded too good to be true, that it sounded like a scam, she looked at me with pity, sorry for my skeptical nature that was going to cost me a golden opportunity. I never asked how much money they ended up investing, but from what I could surmise from various conversations it was a considerable sum, a sum with which they couldn't afford to gamble. After I first heard about the real estate scheme, I started to keep tabs on it online and watched as the proposed properties never developed and more and more investors started filling up message boards wondering where their money went. And as more evidence arose proving it was a scam, the smarter and smugger I felt. But there is a flip side to my smugness.

I have a theory—well, it's more like Shakespeare's theory based on the line from Hamlet, *The lady doth protest too much, methinks.* I think about it often when people rant repeatedly about a subject. Jeff and I used to attend a church with a pastor who always segued into a tirade about the evils of pornography when delivering his sermon. It only took a few sermons before I leaned over to Jeff and whispered, "I think this guy watches a lot of porn." Noticing how other people obsess about an issue they are trying to hide from, or are blind to, makes me sometimes wonder, because I am so attracted to stories about scams, *Where is my blind spot? Where am I being scammed?* And now I finally know, and I haven't just been scammed; I've been the scammer as well and I don't know whether to feel disgusted at myself for falling for it or be impressed with how long I cleverly strung myself along.

This isn't the first time I've realized that I've fallen for a long con. I had the same kind of realization about a year and a half ago when I watched *Embrace: The Documentary,* which follows body image activist Taryn Brumfitt as she explores the pervasive culture of body hating and what she believes is the cure: body acceptance. Her mission started when she posted a before-and-after picture of herself on Facebook. Except, unlike most before-and-after pictures, the before picture featured her posing on stage in a sparkling silver bikini during a bodybuilding competition after she spent fifteen weeks of working out, sometimes twice a day, and restricting her calories. She said getting to that weight and level of fitness was difficult work, meant a lot of sacrifices, and left her grumpy. At the competition, she observed that all of the competitors, despite the fact they had shapes most women would be happy with, were still unsatisfied. They sat backstage pinching the skin of their thighs and stomachs looking for villainous fat and making critical comments about their size and shape, just like most women do.

Taryn's after picture showed her sitting naked after her body returned to its natural shape and size after she stopped the intense workouts and calorie restriction. The difference? Her happiness, her level of contentment, her ease in the world. Taryn tells the interviewer, "It's not your body that needs to change, it's your perspective. Your body is not an ornament, it is a vehicle to your dreams."

That line, and in fact, the whole documentary, shook me. At the time, I had been spending an inordinate amount of time and physical and mental energy worrying about what my body looked like, how much food I put into it and how much exercise I thought it needed to keep it from getting bigger. I didn't focus on it because it was a fun project, because I enjoyed portion planning, because I liked always being sore from exercise and being a slave to my fitness tracker. I did it because I thought that is what I was supposed to do because it seemed to be the female mandate. Because being fat, getting fat, was the worst thing that could happen. And being thin was the best. I'd never heard the message that my body was good enough, just as it is, right now. I didn't realize I had a choice to not want to try to be skinny.

Those ninety minutes of watching *Embrace* was a turning point. I went to the library and checked out books on body acceptance and registered for online body acceptance programs. One of the first exercises in one of the courses was to examine my daily thought cycle about my weight and body. This is what I wrote:

> Wake up-body check: pinch belly, thighs, upper arms to calibrate level of fatness—go to the bathroom then undress completely and weigh myself. If both of these morning tests are acceptable, I feel good about my body, but then the worry sets in that I won't be able to maintain it. If both the morning tests are unacceptable, then I feel bad about my body and panic that I am on the path to obesity. Both results lead me to commit to having a good day eating and exercising. I over-exercise to the point of soreness and injury. I don't pay attention to hunger signals and faithfully count and restrict my calories so I will have enough left for dinner. I try to stay under my calorie needs but am always thinking about the next *allowable* snack, the next meal. I feel tired and grumpy. I get discouraged that I didn't eat less through the day. I panic I won't be

able to get through the rest of the day and stay under my calorie goal. I have a glass of wine to deal with anxiety over eating before dinner and then feel guilty about the extra calories. Wine weakens my resolve and I overeat at dinner, but I still don't feel satisfied, and I graze after dinner and obsess about what I can have for an allowable evening snack. I finally break down and eat a snack that puts me over my calorie goal. I feel like a failure. I eat some more and feel uncomfortable. I am disgusted, ashamed, and angry at myself. I make a new plan for the next day and vow to stick to it.

After watching *Embrace,* I made a new plan. To stop worrying about the shape of my body, to stop counting calories, to stop weighing myself, to stop exercising and moving in ways that don't serve me. I gave myself eighteen months for it to work, for the body-hating thoughts to fall away. I don't know where I came up with the number. Maybe it came from a personal testimony I read. But I told myself: read the books, follow the course, do the work, and give yourself eighteen months. I did, and it worked. It started working almost from the beginning, and even though there were some setbacks, my body image and body acceptance continually improved. My judgement of my body began to wane. My mind began to clear. I broke the cycle. I stopped weighing myself. I ate what I wanted, when I wanted, and however much I wanted (there were a lot of donuts and pizza consumed that first summer). I went up a size and had to buy new pants, but instead of going down a shame spiral, I felt liberated, knowing gaining weight doesn't mean I'm a failure. It doesn't mean anything. Instead, I thought about how I want to feel, not what shape I think I should be. And it was a relief.

My meeting with Val about my *life event* occurred about eighteen months after I began my body acceptance journey. I wonder if, having let go of a body image problem, which had plagued me since my early teens, a part of my brain (I'm looking at you, my shadow) determined that now it was time to work on other things plaguing me. That if I could accept my body, maybe I could start to accept something else.

I'm not sure if there is someone somewhere in the hidden regions of my brain (main suspect being my shadow), with some sort of master plan, but my eighteen months of working towards body acceptance is serving another purpose. Because I was able to change my body image, and because my *body in the backyard* dream changed after less than a week of practising Levine's exercise, I believe I don't have to continue to endure the patterns and cycles that have kept me from fully appreciating all the blessings in my life, that healing is possible and available to me. And even though the idea of changing three decades of coping is overwhelming, it doesn't seem hopeless.

So, I make a pact with myself. I give myself eighteen months. Not to be completely healed, not to be perfectly at ease, content, or happy, but just to spend less energy on coping strategies, and more time living fully. I tell myself I don't have to reach a particular goal; all I have to do is try.

7

It's late November, sixteen days since my meeting with Val, and I'm in the locker room at work peeling off winter layers and changing into my police issue uniform, trying to avoid the wet spots on the floor left by my thawing boots.

Jill strolls into the change room and gives me a smile that lets me know she's got my back, which I'm grateful for because even though I'm over the initial shock, the tidal wave of emotion, I still feel shaky, fragile, like an overinflated balloon ready to pop at the slightest touch. I'm worried I'm not yet resilient enough to take a tough call, but I don't think I need to be at home either. I want to start getting back to my regular routine.

It wasn't my lifelong dream to work in Communications for a police department or to work outside the home for that matter. For eleven years I stayed at home, homeschooling Maddie and Max and taking care of the house. For the last three of those years, I worked part-time writing for TV documentaries for local producers (no, you haven't seen any of the shows).

My husband, Jeff, wrote full-time for television, and therein lay the problem. Having two writers in the family was putting all our eggs in one basket. Having two Saskatchewan television writers in the family was like throwing the eggs on the floor. Jeff made a good income when there was work, but every spring, when the workload slowed down, I panicked and started cruising through the want ads. And every spring I was faced with the harsh reality that a Bachelor of Arts in Russian (don't ask why and no, I can't speak it) doesn't qualify me for much more than an eleven-dollar-an-hour job at Tim Hortons.

I didn't have an issue with working at a coffee shop: work is work. But a minimum wage job didn't make it worthwhile for Jeff to take less writing work to look after the house and kids while I was away.

The first time I heard about the Communications position was from my friend Lisa. "The pay is great. Plus, with shift work, I work four days on and then have four days off."

The pay and work schedule sounded perfect for our life. Jeff could write on my days off and then take care of the kids and home while I worked. After eleven years at home, I had let my life become a bit myopic and was feeling burned out from the all-important but mostly thankless job of being a stay-at-home mom. I did a sit-along with Lisa to find out what the job was like and knew almost immediately it would be a good fit for me. I applied for an open position and, to my surprise, got it. And now, ten years later, I still think it's a good fit.

Our Communications Centre consists of two rooms. One is the call-taking room, where we answer two separate lines: the non-emergency police line and 911. It has eight workstations, each one outfitted with a computer, two keyboards and three monitors. The Sergeant's workstation is on a raised podium at the back and the dispatch room joins to the front of the call-taking room with double sliding doors. Dispatch has three workstations, but usually only two people work in there. There are nine special constables on my platoon and we take turns rotating through call-taking and dispatching each shift.

At work, I don't think anyone needs to hear my story, but I can't help it and it's during dispatch that I blurt to whoever has the misfortune to be stuck with me. I blurt, not because I want their pity (I don't think) but because I find what happened to me fascinating. Fascinating that I was in complete denial that what happened to me in ninth grade was significant, that it had an impact, that it infected every part of my life.

Fascinating that for the past ten years at work, I never considered what happened to be sexual assault. That I never considered it at all. That for the past ten years, despite receiving information through talks, emails, conferences about the signs and symptoms of trauma I never connected the dots that anything I experienced had anything to do with trauma. That I was completely duped.

That trauma can be sneaky as hell.

I'm lucky, because my co-workers don't dismiss my story. Instead, like Jill, they listen with compassion and support me. When I tell Norrie I went to talk to my therapist about a few calls and *one other little thing*, Norrie nods and says, "It's the little things that will get you." How did I not know that? How did she? I wonder if she knows because a little thing got her.

I'm lucky. We have a new sergeant this block, and I ask him if I can talk to him privately.

I tell him I had a mental health setback, but I don't describe it. I don't tell my story. I tell him about my bipolar diagnosis. I usually tell my sergeants this. I want them to know about it in case I start exhibiting strange behaviour or work habits. In case I might need intervention. I've always believed I am at the low end of the bipolar spectrum, but not confident I will stay there. I worry some incident, some hormonal change, some chemical imbalance will push me over the edge, out of control. There but for the grace of God.

My sergeant nods when I tell him this. He tells me about how his co-workers noticed changes in him, which prompted him to get mental health help. He tells me about how a female friend is bipolar and has been recently struggling with a #MeToo revelation. The connection is not lost on me.

I'm shaky the whole first block of work, but what I am learning firsthand about trauma is giving me perspective with my callers. Judgementalism is an occupational hazard in my job. It's easy for me to take a phone call from a person at their worst, on their worst day, and think I know who they are. It's easy to think the mother who swears and then hangs up on the EMS dispatcher who is trying to give CPR instructions to help save her baby might not love her child. It's easy to judge the person who lets the abusive ex-partner with the restraining order back in the house as not wanting to help themselves. But now, my perspective is starting to shift.

I take a call from a male whose roommate has overdosed on fentanyl. Because they both realize they can easily die from a fentanyl overdose they made a safety plan involving putting their naloxone in a safe place. But now he can't remember where that safe place is. While one part of me thinks the situation has the makings of a dark comedy sketch, the better part of me thinks about the mindset of knowing a drug is powerful enough to kill you and risk taking it anyway.

I've struggled with understanding addiction, with how it is described as a disease. I've thought it's unfair to lump addiction in with diseases like cancer and MS. Unfair to think that a person with type 1 diabetes has just as much choice about having their disease as an alcoholic. At the same time, I understand what a hold addiction has on people.

When my children were young and asked me what I would do if I caught them smoking, I told them the story of Jeff's father, their grandfather, who died five years before I met Jeff. Jeff was living at home with his parents while his dad was dying from lung cancer, most likely brought on by smoking more than a pack of cigarettes a day for over thirty years. One day while Jeff was giving him a shave, his dad talked about how he yearned for a cigarette, the very thing responsible for his illness. He died the next day. I told my children the story to illustrate the powerful hold of addiction, but my subtext was always: *it's hard to quit after you choose to start taking addictive substances.*

Addiction is one of the coping methods listed on Val's pages. I put shopping under that category, but I don't consider it in the same universe as a chemical addiction and even though I had been numbing with ibuprofen and wine, I was pretty sure it wouldn't morph into anything stronger, mostly because too much of either doesn't agree with me and I don't like the feeling of being out of control while intoxicated. I was right. As I started to feel better, I stopped the daily wine and ibuprofen.

I think about all the other coping methods I checked off. I think about choice. All of the coping methods I use seem like they could be choices. Maybe I could have chosen not to minimize what happened. Maybe I could have chosen not to chase boys. Maybe I could choose to just stop shopping. Maybe I could choose to stay present in my body and not disconnect. Maybe I could just choose to relax and not be super-alert. Maybe I could choose to be content and not have to look for problems to fix. Maybe I could just choose to not have suicidal thoughts. Maybe I could just choose to enjoy intimacy. Maybe I could just choose to trust people enough to have lasting friendships.

The problem is I don't remember deciding to make these choices. I don't remember any handout in health class entitled "Top 25 Methods of Coping with a Potential Traumatic Incident" and then ticking off fifteen of them as if it was a choose-my-own-adventure novel. Not only did I not remember making those choices, I didn't even know what I was doing was coping to deal with the trauma of sexual abuse. Not until now. And now, I'm just grasping why I needed to cope. What feelings I was protecting myself from. What truth I couldn't face. And now, even with the beginnings of the knowledge, even though the waves of shock are subsiding, even though I'm feeling better, I'm still finding myself using my automatic methods of coping to get by, because while I now see the damage, just knowing about it, accepting it, doesn't fix it. And until I find more strategies that work, more tools to unwind the last two-thirds of my life, I'm stuck with coping. Because right now I don't know how to switch it off. I don't know how to stop doing all of those things and not feel like the volcano bubbling inside of me is not going to erupt and blow me to pieces.

I'm still on the 911 line, listening to my caller with the overdosing friend, while the ambulance dispatcher attempts to gather information and the caller frantically searches his apartment for the safe place they'd stashed their naloxone, and I don't see weakness. I don't see choice. Because now I understand that if I didn't choose my coping methods, neither did he, and I wonder what kind of pain he is trying to protect himself from to risk taking a drug so poisonous that he keeps the antidote close at hand.

In *Waking the Tiger*, Levine provides a long list of examples of events that may cause unresolved trauma. In addition to sexual, physical and emotional abuse, it includes things I never would have associated with the word *trauma*: loss of a loved one, illness and accidents, routine surgery and dental procedures. Levine explains his list is not exhaustive and says that throughout his long career of working with patients, the scope of experiences that can result in unresolved trauma has surprised him. I'm surprised at his list too. I never before considered that the effects of trauma could be so widespread. But now, in my first block back at work, I see it.

I see trauma in the homeless person stealing sanitizer gel from the hospital in order to get his alcohol fix. In the seventy-year-old woman who lives in a tiny house so filled with her hoardings that she needs to crawl through a tunnel of her stacked garbage to get out the front door to meet the officer dispatched to take a report from her. In the woman whose throat was slit by her partner and after he served his time for attempted murder, she took him back. I see it, and even though I don't understand it, I see it as a pattern of coping and I wonder: what are they protecting themselves from? Do they know? I see it and I realize how lucky I am. Because their methods of coping are on the list, but I didn't check them off. My coping is easier to hide. My coping has allowed me to stay safe and healthy, and it wasn't because I chose it to be that way, it was only a matter of luck.

8

I t's been four weeks since my last meeting with Val, and I'm back in the waiting room outside her office listening to Mariah Carey belt out "All I Want for Christmas Is You," which is acceptable since it is now December. I watch the fish wriggle after each other in the aquarium and glance sadly at the toys on the bookshelf, thinking no child deserves to feel what I've been feeling. Wondering how their little bodies can withstand it.

Twitch. Ribbit. Stretch.

I don't want to be here. I don't think I can take another revelation, but I don't know what else to do. I can't do this on my own. I have people I can talk to, people who will listen and sympathize, but it's not enough. I need a person who is trained, who has experience, who understands and can guide me.

I notice my breathing is shallow. I take a deep breath. My belly and chest fully expand. It's been two weeks since the python slithered away and it hasn't come back since.

Val invites me into her office. I sit in the same corner of the same couch. She asks about my plans for Christmas, checking to see if the season is generally more stressful for me.

I tell her it usually isn't. What I don't tell her is that Christmas is one of the victims of my years of fixing. That it takes me ten minutes to put out our handful of decorations and other than that I do very little else.

She then asks me how I've been doing. I try to explain the aftershock of our last meeting: the confusion, the crying, the suicidal thoughts, the wonderment of how I never knew.

"Sometimes these things just bubble up when we're ready." Val raises her hand while wiggling her fingers to represent bubble rising to a surface.

"Bubble up? More like a mushroom cloud." I make a fist in front of me then explode my fingers open.

"Or like a mushroom cloud." Val cocks her head and smiles her affirmation.

I lean forward, forearms on thighs, hands clasped. "Was what happened to me really that bad?"

She raises her eyebrows, grabs a paper from her bookshelf and rolls her chair closer to me.

"I want you to have a look at this." She shows me an outline of a body. Inside the body are lines and shapes representing the brain, heart, lungs, stomach, nerves and blood vessels. Around the body are phrases and sentences.

"When a person feels threatened, their amygdala is activated." She points to her head just behind her ear. "This is the part of the brain that is in charge of the fight, flight and freeze reflex. It's instinctual, you have no control over it. Each time it is activated there are physical changes that happen in your body." She points to the body parts and explains the physical changes: "Our breathing gets shallow and speeds up. We release chemicals like adrenaline into the body. We start sweating. Our digestion slows down, causing us to feel queasy. The mind and body become alert and focuses on pain and potential threats. The mouth becomes dry. Our muscles tense up, preparing us to fight or run away."

I nod along as she goes through the list. I've seen some of this before. It's good information. Good to know. But it doesn't answer my question.

Val looks at me, nodding away like I've just heard the soup of the day and dinner specials from a waiter. "Karin, you said this boy grabbed you repeatedly."

I nod, waiting for the waiter to go through the drink specials.

"Your body would have perceived that as a threat."

Still nodding, waiting for her to move on so I can look at the menu.

"This, all of this"—she points at the body outline and menu of symptoms—"would have happened to you every time."

"Wait, what?" I jerk my head to attention. "That would have happened to me every time?"

Her time to nod.

I screw my mouth up and consider this. I was pretty sure my body reacted that way at least the first few times, the times I remember vividly, but wouldn't I have gotten used to it by then? I consider asking her how she knows it would have happened every time. Then my mouth falls open as it hits me. I don't have to ask her how she knows, because I know. I know I know because I have that physical reaction every time I talk about what the boy did, every time I think about it, every time I'm assaulted with the image of it. And I realize, my body never got used to the boy grabbing and groping me. My body perceived what he did to me as a threat every single time.

I start to realize something else. I've been thinking that what is wrong with me is a purely mental health problem. That because I'm weaker mentally, I just can't handle a little thing like a boy goofing around in class. That the problem isn't *what* happened to me, the problem *is* me. But what if that is not the case? What if, because I had a physical reaction so often, it is a physical injury? A nervous system injury? Is there such a thing? Is there a cure? A treatment? Can I get a nerve transplant, say, from a Buddhist monk donor? Can a doctor graft the monk's nerve onto mine so it can grow and re-regulate my whole system? I like the idea of the quick fix, but I'm pretty sure it doesn't exist. Even if it did, if I don't qualify for a service dog, I'm sure not going to qualify for a Buddhist monk nerve transplant.

I look at the outline of the body, the sentences around it. I take it in.

"Why didn't I tell anyone?" I look up at Val.

Val doesn't hesitate, "You told the most powerful person you knew."

My hands wave her reasoning away. "But why didn't I tell anyone else?"

"What was your teacher's reaction when you told him?"

I shrug my shoulders, forearms outstretched, palms facing up. "Nothing."

"Nothing," Val confirms, "and why?"

I shrug again.

"Maybe because he just thought boys will be boys?" She raises her eyebrows.

"That's it!" I remember the look on the teacher's face, his demeanour, his body language, all telling me without words that he can't stop a boy from being a boy.

Boys will be boys. Is that what restraining a girl, feeling her breasts, grabbing her crotch, groping her bottom is? Just boys will be boys? If that's the case, then where does that leave girls? If boys will be boys, then does it follow that girls will be toys? I think about that teacher. I think about him giving the boy a hall pass to repeatedly grope me, and I'm starting to get angry at him.

I sit back in Val's couch. "Why didn't I tell my parents?"

"What do you think your parents would have done?"

Val leans back in her chair.

"I don't know."

I remember my phone call with Steve a few weeks ago.

After I told him my story, he told me one of his own. When he was fourteen and working at the local grocery store, a man from town started to regularly engage him in friendly conversations, started to take an interest in him. One day the man gave Steve a ticket to the Fire Department's pig roast. Dad found out about the ticket, asked Steve where he got it, wanted to know who gave it to him. The pig roast was close enough for Steve to ride his bike, but my dad insisted on driving him. At the roast, Dad asked Steve to point out the man who gave him the ticket. Steve did. Dad walked over to the man, had a conversation with him and the man never approached Steve again.

Dad served in the Marines. He has large service tattoos on each bicep. He worked three years as a police officer, before I was born. He's not tall, but he's muscular. He looks like a man who can handle himself. A man you don't want to find out what will happen if you cross him. He's a man who doesn't feel like he has to raise his voice to get his point across. He doesn't have to work to intimidate, doesn't have to posture. All he has to do is have a conversation. I've always thought of him as my first line of defence if anything ever happened. My second line would be my brothers, who take after my dad. My third line of defence is my sister and god help you if you make it through the other two lines and have to deal with her. And if my sister can't take care of you, then a stern look of disapproval from my mom will wither you to your core. So why didn't I tell my dad? Why didn't I tell any of them?

I tell Val Steve's story. What Dad did for Steve. I tell her I'd like to think my dad would have helped me too. What I don't tell her is that I'm not sure he would have. Because if *a very moral man* didn't think what happened was wrong, worthy of intervention, that it was just *boys will be boys*, would my dad?

We move on. Val wants to talk about my suicidal thoughts. I don't know why it's such an issue. I've already told her I'm not going to do it.

"Do you know who usually finds the body?"

I try to think back to all the suicide calls I've taken. Sometimes it's a landlord. My friend Mirjana had a basement suite tenant who hanged herself: it was the cable guy who found her. Most times it's a family member. Val answers before I can sort through my file to come up with the most accurate answer.

"It's children. Children usually find the body."

Part of me is skeptical that, based on the calls I've taken, this is a statistically accurate statement; another part of me decides this isn't a point I need to debate right now. Instead, I nod at the gravity of her words.

"It's the children." She looks pointedly at me.

Okay, I get it, I think to myself and nod again to appease her. But then it starts to sink in. Maddie and Max still live at home. It's very likely, if I suicided at home, they would find me. I start to feel sick to my stomach. I think about the people I've talked to: the parents who found a suicide note from their daughter before the police found her body in a remote area outside of the city. The wife whose husband suicided on their bed. The mother woken up by her young daughter, who had discovered her sister hanging in their bedroom closet. The sound of their despair is nothing like I've heard any actor capture on screen. It comes from a place only the shock of their reality can tap. It reaches through the phone and taps me in the same place. I don't want it for my children, for Jeff.

"Do you have a safety plan if you feel that way again?"

"I'm not going to do it." I narrow my eyes and shake my head at her.

"But do you have a plan?" she presses. "What would you do?"

I hunch my shoulders up to my ears and look at the ceiling for inspiration, for something I can tell her to end this line of questioning so we can move on.

"I guess I would call Mobile Crisis."

But I wouldn't. I wouldn't call anyone in that moment. The thought of it is abhorrent. I've only told a handful of people about my suicide attempt, and I never tell anyone when I am having a suicidal thought. Telling someone about the thought while I am having it seems worse than the thought itself. I'm not sure why. As a 911 call-taker I've talked to many people who call because they are having suicidal thoughts. I'm not glad they are having the thoughts, but I'm glad they call, because then I can send someone to help.

Years ago, I took a call from a man calling from a pay phone. He said he was going to suicide but that when police found his body, he would have his cell phone on him and in his phone would be the name of a friend to notify about his death. While he talked, I quickly typed up a high priority call to send police to the location of the pay phone. I asked him questions, trying to stall.

"I know what you're trying to do," he said, "but I've made up my mind. I'm hanging up now."

"Wait! At least tell me what your name is so we will know your identity when we find you."

He told me his name and hung up. Police checked the area of the pay phone, but it was at the crowded downtown bus terminal. With no description of the male, it was impossible to find him, even if he was still there. I did a search for his name on our system. I found three males with the same name for whom we also had cell phone numbers. I called them all. The first two numbers were out of service. A man answered the third.

"You found my number." He sounded surprised.

"Yeah." I breathed a sigh of relief. "I got lucky."

I tried to convince him to tell me where he was. He wouldn't. I tried to get him to talk to a Mobile Crisis counsellor, or our police crisis negotiator. He just wanted to talk to me.

It was at a time when we were only able to get the nearest cell tower when pinging a cell phone, so there was no other way to find his location. He wasn't planning on dying at home. He wanted to die somewhere with a view of the river. He planned to overdose.

An officer located his family, got his description, the kind of vehicle he might be driving, where he might go. Even with all of that information, finding someone who doesn't want to be found isn't easy. People think the police have a crystal ball. We don't.

My sergeant notified a crisis negotiator, who sat by my side, giving me tips. I was out of my depth. The caller told me what kind of drugs he was taking. The negotiator left the room, made a call, came back and passed me a note.

"My co-worker just made a call to a doctor," I told my caller. "He says the drugs you took are strong enough to kill you. And I'm just worried that, as the drugs take effect, you won't be able to get the help you need if you change your mind, so now is the time to tell me where you are."

I told him this because I know some people are relieved their attempts didn't work, like me. And some people change their mind when it is too late. When I was dispatching one winter, a call came in about a woman on a bridge. Saskatchewan winters can be brutal, getting down to -40° Celsius. When Jeff told me that before I moved here, I asked him what -40 Celsius was in Fahrenheit. "Minus forty. It's where Celsius and Fahrenheit meet," he said. The air gets so cold in the winter that plumes of moisture evaporate from the river, sometimes clouding the bridges above the deathly cold river. Ice creeps out from the bank, but the river moves too fast for it to freeze completely.

The caller indicated they thought the female was going to jump. I read out the call and dispatched officers. One officer made it to the bridge within a minute and confirmed he had eyes on the female, and she was preparing to jump. He tried to intervene. He tried to get there in time, but she was too fast, too decisive.

"She jumped!" the officer yelled into the radio.

My stomach dropped. My co-worker radioed the fire department to request they dispatch their rescue boat. I dispatched other officers to get into position along the river and on other nearby bridges. The officer on scene called out the colour of the female's coat, to help officers along the river spot her. It's not uncommon for officers to attempt a water rescue themselves, when the weather is warm, if the person is closer to shore. But she jumped from the middle of the bridge. The river is too fast and too cold for anyone, other than trained rescue divers wearing the proper equipment, to attempt a rescue.

"Her head is above water," the officer on scene called out. "She's trying to swim towards the ice. She's at the ice, she's trying to hold on to it."

At the edge of my chair, I updated the call, waiting for the officer to say that she had got a hold of the ice. She was pulling herself up. She was safely on the ledge.

"She can't get a grip." The officer yelled, "She's gone under. I can't see her now."

I waited patiently for updates, hoping other officers would spot her as the river carried her away. A sergeant asked for updates from officers on scene.

"Nothing from the east side of the river."

"Nothing from the west side of the river."

"Nothing from University Bridge."

All eyes stayed on the river. My eyes stayed on my overhead GPS map showing the location of the officers. The fire department arrived and put their boat in the water. Officers stayed at their posts, looking for any sign of her while the boat scoured the river. They didn't find her.

"I'm not going to change my mind," my suicidal male caller said.

"You don't know that." I envisioned the woman clawing at the ice ledge, trying to get a grip.

"You don't have to change your mind." My voice softened. "But you also don't have to do this today. This decision, it's forever, you can never change it."

"The view here is beautiful...my phone is dying...I'm starting to get sleepy."

"Please tell me where you are."

"Sorry."

He never told me where he was, and our officers never found him. Our conversation ended four hours after I first answered his call on 911. I didn't sleep well that night. My mind raced with all of the things I should have said. The next morning at work I checked the file on the male. He was never located. Later in the day the crisis negotiator walked into Communications.

"I wanted to let you know, I just heard that male from yesterday checked himself into the hospital last night. He's doing okay."

My shoulders finally relaxed from the tension they'd been holding since I first answered the call and I took what felt like my first breath in twenty-two hours. Later that day, he called me again, but this time to say thanks. I told him I was glad he went to the hospital; glad I could help. I meant it. I would do it for anyone. So why won't I let anyone do it for me?

"I'll call Mobile Crisis if it ever gets that bad again," I repeat and look meaningfully at Val.

"Okay, good." She leans back. I think I'm off the hook but then she asks me what my other options would be. If there is anyone else I could call. I do a mental rundown of who I could bear to tell. Only one person comes to mind.

"Jeff, I could talk to Jeff about it."

Val seems satisfied with my safety plan and we move on. She talks more about the nervous system and offers strategies to help regulate it: grounding, self-soothing, breathing. She gives me examples of each. We practise a few. She asks me to clap my hands together really hard. We do it together. Then she asks me to notice the sensation in my hands, to stay with the sensation until it goes away. And I feel it, I'm there in my hands, noticing it, paying attention, feeling tiny sparks shoot all around the surface of my palms. I think this is what is meant by mind-body connection. I'm starting to get it. Val and I sit there, palms up, feeling the sparks begin to fade.

"It lasts a long time, doesn't it?" Val glances from me to her own hands.

"Yeah."

I don't think I've ever sat with a feeling like that before without my mind launching off the top of my head. But now I'm sitting there, watching my hands, curious about what is happening, calm. My time is up. I made it through the session. I make another appointment to see Val next month.

9

It's grocery shopping day. A week after my second meeting with Val, when she showed me the outline of the body with the nerves and words, I'm starting to notice how distracted I am. How unfocused. With the looming task of grocery shopping ahead, I'm unable to do anything else, think about anything else, or make decisions. I notice how long it takes me to work up the nerve to start getting ready to leave the house. How my mind pre-emptively leaves my orbit before I even walk out the door. I notice how I stand in the entrance of our house, shoes on, taking shallow breaths, stalling. I think about how this is a pattern. A pattern Jeff and the kids have noticed and commented on. A pattern that usually has them waiting in the car while I perform little stalling tasks, until I screw up the courage to join them. It's not checking to see if the stove is off eight times, tapping the light switch and the doorknob in a certain pattern. It's a more subtle variation on the theme. Check pockets for a tissue. Go to the bathroom mirror to check my teeth. Grab my purse. Go to my bedroom mirror to check how I look in my clothes. Get my keys. Check my pocket for a tissue. Check if the back door is locked. Go to the bathroom one last time, even though I went five minutes ago. Check my hair. Check my pockets for my keys and a tissue. Go to the bedroom. Put on lotion. Put on lip gloss. Check my pockets. Check my purse. Repeat any and all of these until I feel safe enough to leave.

I drive to the store on icy grey streets in my frosted-up red Mazda hatchback. Saskatoon is in the depths of winter darkness and even though it is 8:00 a.m., there is still no sign of the sun. Light posts adorned with holiday lights attempt to lift the spirits, but I am too busy noticing other things to feel their effect. Instead, I notice how I avoid looking at people in the other cars. Trying to pretend I don't notice them watching me, evaluating me. Stoplights are tricky. I try not to stop parallel to another car. I don't want to be in easy eyesight of another driver. But I don't like to be a little in front of them so they can see me. I notice how I never try to park close to the front of the store. How I don't think I deserve it. That it would be presumptuous to try. That other drivers would think, "Who does she think she is, trying to get a close parking spot?" I park further away, telling myself it's because I like to get the extra little walk.

At the grocery store, as I wheel my cart around, pretending to concentrate intently on my shopping list and the items around me, I notice how much I feel noticed. Like a spotlight is shining on me, like there is a target on my back. I try not to notice my heart thumping in my chest, my armpits blooming with sweat, the dizziness from not breathing. I try to act normal. I try to blend in. But I've always been confused about the right way to blend in. I'm always searching for the look that will keep people from noticing me. Even though I don't enjoy fussing with my hair, I look for the perfect hairstyle that looks nice but not too nice. Even though I'm not interested in fashion, I am on a never-ending quest for the perfect wardrobe, the perfect camouflage. To look at me, you wouldn't think I spent much time and money on either my hair or my wardrobe. That's the point.

In the line-up to the checkout, the skin on my back and neck begins to crawl as I feel the person behind me enter my personal space. My ears perk up, waiting for the person to tell me I don't know what I'm doing because I haven't moved my cart up closer to the person in front of me, to admonish me for not pushing my way forward and putting items on the conveyor belt. I notice how the person in front of me is taking her time packing, asking the cashier a question about a price, searching for coins in her purse. I notice how I wonder at her blasé attitude towards the extreme sport of grocery shopping. While the person in front of me takes her time, I feign interest in a magazine featuring the royal family's Christmas plans, pretend to be engrossed in the selection of gum, practise my nonchalant face.

Putting my items on the conveyor belt, I notice the cashier watching me with her peripheral vision, waiting for me to slip up and put the raw meat before the fresh produce, the canned goods after the eggs. *Act natural*, I tell myself. But what is natural? What do people expect me to do while I put items on the conveyor belt? While I pack my bags? Am I supposed to engage in conversation?

I try to think of something to say. But I'm too busy keeping an eye on everybody else that I have little brain space left for chit-chat. Instead, I settle on trying to smile but it comes out as a grimace. My neck knows my smile is all wrong and wants to twitch. *Don't twitch your neck,* I order myself. Twitch-twitch. My throat notices my neck twitched and wants to push out. *Hold in your neck,* I tell myself. Ribbit-ribbit. *It's just grocery shopping,* I tell myself, *just act like a goddamn normal person.* Twitch-twitch-ribbit-stretch—then rub my nose on my shoulder pretending to itch it when I'm really sniffing my armpit to gauge just how offensive I am at this moment.

When I'm packing my groceries, I notice how I scan the other line-ups to see who is watching me, noticing me. I can't tell where the threat is coming from, but I know it's there. I feel it. I hurry as I pack. It's imperative I get out of the way of the next person as soon as possible. Don't get in the way, don't be a bother. Move! Move! Move! Put the bags in the cart. Don't drop anything. Don't you dare drop anything with your shaking hands. Done, finally. Roll the cart towards the door. Oh no, a slow elderly couple ahead of me. A bottleneck at the exit doors. Tell myself: *It's okay, I'm almost there, just a few more minutes and I'll be through those doors.*

In the parking lot I notice how I seem to have lost control of my fine motor skills as I fumble with my keys. I put the bags in the back of the car, feeling all eyes in the parking lot on me, people driving by on the nearby road taking notes on how I'm loading my car all wrong. A car drives behind me slowly. What do they want? My cart? My parking spot? The pressure is now on to pack up faster, to see if someone needs the cart, to give someone the parking spot, to appease them. Cart away, trunk closed, I make it into the driver's seat. My teeth are chattering and my body starts to tremble all over in waves of powerful chills. It lasts for a couple of minutes before it subsides, leaving me spent. I take a deep breath, grateful that the python still hasn't come back. I think about the picture of the outline of the body. I think about the words. I think about my amygdala. I think it's broken. I think, *They have really got to start working on those Buddhist monk nerve transplants.*

I realize my reaction to grocery shopping isn't unique to that situation. It turns out that is my reaction to nearly everything, everyone, everywhere, every time I leave the house. Part of me wonders if reading about trauma has planted the symptoms in my head, that maybe I am too susceptible to resist the power of suggestion. I consider it, but there is too much evidence to the contrary. Over thirty years of evidence. Memories of being at parties, talking to very nice people while my body becomes cold, breaks out in a sweat and then is taken over by waves of shivering and teeth chattering. Memories of my college friend Troy asking, "What's wrong with your neck?" while I twitched and ribbitted. A memory of my brother, Dave, pulling me aside at my parents' combined eightieth birthday party last summer, a small gathering of my parents, siblings and their families.

"Is something wrong? Are you upset about something?" He held me gently by the arm.

"I'm not upset." I shook my head and looked down at my shoes,."I just sometimes have a hard time being around people."

"Even around us?" His eyes went wide with shock.

"Yeah." I looked away from him, wishing I could have pulled off acting normal a little better. Worried I had hurt his feelings. Feeling like a jerk.

I think about the context of when I have these symptoms. I think about what happened to me in ninth grade. And I wonder. I wonder if having a smiling, laughing boy, who otherwise acted nice to me, regularly grab and grope me eroded my faith in my ability to recognize danger. I wonder if having that happen in front of a class of my peers, whom I grew up with, whom I believed I should be safe with, in front of a teacher who was a nice guy, *a very moral man*, who ignored it, eroded my trust that anyone would help me. I wonder if my amygdala defaulted to freezing because I was not able to effectively fight or flee and eroded my confidence that I can protect myself. And I think, if that's the case, if I don't know what danger looks like, if I don't think people will help me, if I don't think I can protect myself, then, to use one of Val's phrases: *it makes sense*. It makes sense that I might perceive most people, places and situations as threatening. That my body might go into high alert and switch into high gear. That it might try to keep me from going at all.

I think about all of the things I've tried over the last few decades. Dance classes, sports, volunteering, clubs. I haven't stuck with any of them very long. I think about clogging dance class last fall and lawn bowling last summer. The group I dance and bowl with are about the least threatening people you could imagine. Most of them are at least ten to thirty years older than me. I can't out-dance or out-bowl them, but I sure as hell could outrun them. But still, I find myself distracted and pacing around the house on the day of the class or club. I have trouble getting out of bed, making decisions, getting stuff done. I'm on edge. And at the class or club my mind hides under a bench, leaving my body on autopilot, trying to act normal, trying to have fun. It leaves me worn out, with low energy the next day, and I drag myself around the house trying to get into gear. I try these things because volunteering, sports, and socializing are supposed to be good for mental health. But it seems to have the opposite effect on me.

Part of me wishes I could go back. Go back to before I knew, before I noticed. A friend of mine in college introduced me to the saying "feel the fear and do it anyway." I'm not sure what fears she meant or where she applied the saying in her life, but I latched onto the phrase. It became a mantra for me, although not for doing something noble, trying something seemingly out of reach. It became a mantra for answering the phone, leaving the house, going to after-work drinks with co-workers. I would feel the fear and my mind would tune out while my body did it anyway. But now the mantra isn't working as well, because now I'm noticing how it feels and recognizing that it probably isn't a normal reaction, and even though I think I'm on the path to recovery, it feels like I'm getting worse.

I think about my symptoms, my broken amygdala. I wonder at the damage and repercussions of the thoughtless actions of a teenage boy. I think about my own thoughtlessness. I think about how one time, in seventh grade gym class, my friends and I teased a girl, not directly to her face, but definitely within hearing distance, calling her a mean name, saying cruel things. I think about how she didn't deserve it, how no one does. I've thought about it a lot over the years, always with a pang of shame that lingers. Now the shame comes with the horror of other thoughts. Thoughts of what damage, what repercussions were the result of my words. I wonder what being verbally abused by a mean group of girls erodes. I think about other kids I grew up with, other unkindnesses bestowed by me. If they were all tallied up, I don't know if it would amount to me being a bully or just sporadically unkind or thoughtless. I don't know that it matters for the person on the receiving end.

I think about unkindness I've witnessed. Kids I didn't help or stand up for. I wonder where the teachers were. Did they notice? Did they care? Did they try to intervene? I don't remember them trying. Maybe there were too many of us, too few of them. Like prison. As long as there is no rioting, everything is okay. I think back to my decision to homeschool Maddie and Max. Part of it was because I admired the relationship Jeff's sister, Trudy, and her husband, Bernie, had with their homeschooled kids. Part of it was because of my memory of teasing the girl in gym class. I believed there would be no one to protect my kids from that kind of behaviour, and no one to correct them if they perpetrated it. Maybe I also thought of ninth-grade shop class and believed that teachers can't keep them safe. Won't keep them safe. Just to be clear, I'm not categorically against public education. I think it's a very good idea. I just don't think our society values children enough to give the school system and teachers enough resources to care for all of the children under their charge the way they deserve to be cared for. I think until we do, six hours, five days a week, one hundred eighty days a year is a lot of time for children to be at the mercy of their peers.

In the middle of February, Saskatchewan is deep into winter. The snow is so cold it screams under your boots each time you take a step. This year in Saskatoon the average windchill for the month will be -39C. But I'm on vacation in Costa Rica with Jeff.

Jeff works in the front office at an auto service station, a job he took after Max and Maddie started attending school and the Saskatchewan film and television industry took a downturn. The station is owned by friends of ours, who gave him the trip as a bonus. It's a group trip, with about forty couples from Saskatchewan who also either own or work at service stations. When Jeff first told me about the trip and asked if I wanted to go, I said no. I had my reasons. An all-inclusive resort, in my opinion, translates to at least two days of diarrhea. I didn't have clothes. We'd need to get shots. It sounded like a hassle. But what I really meant was I didn't think I could do it. I didn't think that in my current state I could do two plane rides and seven days in a group environment. But what kind of ungrateful person turns down a free trip to Costa Rica in the middle of the Saskatchewan winter?

So, I changed my mind and said, "Sure." But with one caveat. Before he accepted the trip, I asked Jeff to talk to his bosses, let them know I'm going through some *stuff*, that I might not be up to mixing with people. To give them a heads-up in case they want to give the trip to a more outgoing couple, a fun couple. Jeff gave them fair warning; they gave him the trip anyway.

So here we are in Costa Rica in a beautiful bungalow on a lush hillside with a view of the sapphire ocean and the sun-heated air warming me through to the centre of my bones. A family of howler monkeys with glossy espresso-coloured fur is visiting us this morning. The baby clings to its mother's back as she swings herself through the branches foraging for the tastiest leaves.

I sit on the balcony, sip coffee, watch their progress and try not to think about the nine hundred dollars' worth of new clothes in my suitcase. The online hunting and purchasing for them took an embarrassing amount of brain space, time and money. *I have enough summer clothes,* I told myself, and for about six hours felt content with what I had, but the internal pressure leading up to the "vacation" was too much and led to an obsessive search for the right camouflage. On the bright side, I resisted the urge to chop off all my hair before coming.

In the afternoon Jeff and I find a semi-quiet spot where I sit in the shade, in clothes I never needed, slathered in sunscreen, drinking water, reading a book.

I'm noticing. I'm noticing how clusters of people, already fast friends from meeting on the plane, on the bus, in the lobby, spend their days lounging at the pool, at the beach. I notice how jealous of them I am. How I wish I knew how to *hang out*, drink all day and get sunburnt.

I sit under an umbrella watching the waves roll towards the shore, I think about my third meeting with Val. I told her what I've been noticing, but not in depth, just that I notice my physical reaction to social interactions. I told her that I suspect I may be an introvert. In a book I read recently, I came across a description of the difference between extroverts and introverts. An extrovert is a person who is recharged by being around people; an introvert is a person who is recharged by being alone. It sounded about right for me. But I'm not sure if it is a result of nature or nurture. I'm not sure if it's because of the boy in my ninth-grade shop class. It may have something to do with me taking after my nana.

Nana is my maternal grandmother. She and Grandpa divorced right after my brother Dave was born. She lived in a three-bedroom house a short bike ride from my parents' home. She worked from home, keeping the books for my dad's store. She waited until the store was closed and all the employees had gone before going down there to get the books. Other than that, she didn't leave the house much. She wore a daily uniform of polyester pants, a long-sleeved shirt and a polyester smock like the cashiers at the store. She ate frozen TV dinners, canned soup, packaged windmill cookies for dessert, and drank Tab. She had a room full of lush green plants and enjoyed the sweet scent of a large patch of lily of the valley out back. She watched *Wheel of Fortune, The Price Is Right* and did crossword puzzles. Her house was tidy, no clutter. Her only friends were her neighbours, Mr. and Mrs. Dull (I kid you not). She wasn't much of a talker. Not much of a smiler. She lived a small life. A quiet life. A life that I often think about running away to, so much so that I have recurring dreams of living in her house with its massive yard and block-long driveway. In my dream I'm looking for a secret passage, a secret room, a safe room in which to hide within a quiet and predictable home. I don't know if it was a life Nana cultivated out of choice, or coping, or a mixture of both. I don't know if instead of sitting at home, eating her frozen dinner of turkey breast with gravy, mashed potatoes and cherry cobbler she didn't long to live in the world a little more. I don't know that if I had never taken that shop class in high school, I would still idealize her quiet, simple, nearly people-less life.

I tell Val this and she makes a motion with her hands. One hand represents introversion, the other represents trauma. She presses her hands together and says something about the significance of them being fused. I don't remember exactly what she said, but my later interpretation of it is: double whammy. But Val doesn't say it's bad. She doesn't trade in words like good or bad, wrong or right. Her currency is what might make sense and what can be helpful. She tells me the world is made for and admires extroverts. She gives me permission not to be one. She tries to give me a strategy for social situations.

"One thing you can do is try to picture people who support you right here." Val holds her cupped hand, representing a head, up to her shoulder.

I nod and raise my eyebrows to suggest I'll consider it. But my passive response isn't going to cut it with her.

Val raises her own eyebrows. "Who could you imagine?"

I shrug.

Val doesn't take no answer for an answer.

"I don't know. My mom, I guess." I throw out my hands, palms up. Trying to give a right answer. Knowing my mom would fit the bill.

"Good, who else?"

"Jeff?"

"Who else?"

I shrug my shoulders again, not because I can't come up with people who I think should be on my shoulder, but because I don't believe anyone—including my mom and Jeff—would help me, stand up for me, fight for me, if push came to shove. But I sit there and give Val obvious answers, because I want to be a good client, and because I don't think I can say out loud how much I don't believe in the people who, I know in my head, love me.

Thankfully Val moves on to other strategies. She reminds me I have options, that I don't have to attend social situations and if I do, I don't have to stay.

"You could plan to go to a party and just stay five minutes." Val gives a little grin.

"Five minutes?" That's ridiculous. Who goes to a party for just five minutes?

She cocks her head to the side and raises her eyebrows and smiles. "It's an option."

I put the suggestion in my back pocket. She gives me some other strategies and also suggests some mantras for when I'm around people. She prefers me to come up with my own, but she gives me some examples.

"They are not them." Val clasps her hands on her lap. "Now is not then." She places her hands palms down on her thighs.

I feel a gentle spread of warmth in my chest. The phrases aren't like positive thinking phrases I'd heard before. Phrases I tried, but couldn't fool myself into believing. Val's phrases sound like truth. They feel like an adjustment to the lens with which I view my world. I put them in my back pocket too.

I don't have time to tell Val this, but I'm also noticing other things. Not necessarily things happening right now. I notice what an anomaly my ninth-grade experience was. How the majority of my interactions with boys, men, people, are neutral or positive. How the evidence of *what is* far outweighs the evidence of *what was.* I notice that people have helped me.

Like one winter when I was driving to visit a friend in another city, my car broke down on the highway. A man stopped to help and gave me a ride to an auto shop in the nearest town. I often think back to that day and consider how lucky I was he stopped to assist me and not for any other reason. Thinking about it now reminds me that most people are decent. Most people are helpful.

I also notice that the boy didn't train all of the fight out of me. I remember being at a school dance in Australia when a boy repeatedly grabbed my butt and I repeatedly told him to knock it off. After the third grab, I swung around and punched him in the gut so hard he fell to the ground with the wind knocked out of him. I also remember the summer after I graduated from university, when I took a walk near the townhouses where I was living, and two men in a moving truck catcalled me. After I got home, I called the moving company to report them. The woman who answered the phone made me repeat what I said twice, and clearly outraged, assured me that it would be handled. Thinking about it now, I wonder if she was in a relationship with one of the men.

I think about where I work. The calls I take. And I notice. Someone once asked, because of my job, if I thought the world was going to hell in a handbasket. I understood where his sentiment was coming from, but I couldn't entirely agree. Because while I hear some of the worst of human behaviour, I also hear the best. The people who have called because they're worried about a homeless person passed out in a snowbank. The teenage girl who pleaded with a stranger on the bridge not to jump. The ex-con who lived in a basement suite, calling to report the five-year-old being abused by her parents upstairs. I've talked to a grandma who takes care of her ten grandchildren by herself. People who let near-strangers stay on their couch because they have nowhere else to go. A woman who found forty dollars in a parking lot outside a Dollar Store and stayed there for two hours waiting for the owner to come back for it. I talk to people more generous, more compassionate and kinder than myself every day.

They are not them; now is not then.

As the sun makes its way across the bright blue Costa Rican sky, its rays creep across my legs. I watch people laugh and drink by the pool. Other people have taken up chairs beside me. I notice my body's automatic reactions: I feel the spotlight overhead, the target on my back. I tell myself *They are not them; now is not then.* I've come up with others as well. *I'm an adult now*, I remind myself, *I know how to protect myself.*

Sometimes I say the mantras and they roll off my back. Sometimes they absorb into my skin. I start to recognize the difference between my body perceiving threat and the chances of there actually being a threat. I notice I feel a little better between social interactions. I dread them a little less. I recover a little faster. Jeff and I go on walks. We paddleboard and kayak in the ocean. We take dips in the pool. Meet some people. Have a few breakfasts with his bosses. We get diarrhea for a few days, but it's not too bad.

A part of me still wishes I were the type of person to hang out by the pool, nursing an all-day buzz, but I'm starting to give myself permission to be who I am, where I am, right now.

10

The bitter cold of February begins to abate in March. But not much. While the promise of spring breeds optimism in people in other places, people who live Saskatchewan know better. We've been swiped by the paw of March's winter lion too many times to hold faith in a few relatively warm days. Still, it doesn't leave us entirely hopeless that this year there will be no spring, no summer. We cling to the subtle changes: the fading of deep snow ruts on the side streets, the appearance of self-appointed neighbourhood block captains filled with purpose and determination as they chip away at the ice blocking storm drains. And just like the weather, things are changing, shifting for me as well. I'm sweating less and when I do it smells less offensive and ruins fewer shirts. Decades of persistent neck and shoulder pain and discomfort are mostly gone. My neck twitches, throat ribbits and mouth stretches are waning. More of my dreams have changed. In my fighting dream it doesn't feel like a battle to the death. Instead, I fight and defend myself with calm and control. I wake up feeling curious and neutral, instead of threatened and distressed. I have another dream, a verbal confrontation dream, in which, instead of feeling out of control and defensive, I'm able to express my point of view dispassionately and with a measured voice. I find in real life, I'm more able to mimic the dream, and have conversations and disagreements without getting personally invested in them, without feeling that something is at stake if the other person doesn't agree with me. I still catch myself shallow breathing, but I can reclaim my full breath if I try, and the python is still MIA. I can't remember the last time I had a suicidal thought.

At work I feel less suspicious of others, more open. Instead of sitting at one of the outside, more secluded work-stations, I choose to sit on the inside more often. I participate in more conversations, become more curious about my co-workers, start to enjoy the social interaction. I'm also a little more resilient to interpersonal workplace conflict. I don't take things as personally and if I do, I don't hold onto it for as long or retreat completely into my shell. I find that with my callers, I've softened. Taking all the calls I've taken, it's not hard for me to imagine the endless ways in which people are exposed to trauma, and the myriad ways they may cope with it, so I'm a little less judgemental when our conversations don't go the way I expect.

I'm also a little more sensitive to my callers' experiences. A young mother called me from her house to report that thirty minutes before, she was waiting at a bus stop when a man who seemed high, intoxicated, mentally unstable or all three walked her way. She retreated into the bus shelter for safety, but he followed her in, cornered her, pulled out a knife and held it up in front of her, then eventually walked away.

"I tried to get out of his way, I tried to make myself small." Her tone of voice sounded like she was trying to convince me that she made an attempt to avoid being his target, as if she was somehow responsible. "He didn't say anything or threaten me," she minimized, "but when I got home and told my husband, he said I should report it."

She sounded like she thought she might be overreacting, wasting my time, that it wasn't worth reporting to the police because she wasn't hurt. But she also sounded shaken up.

I explained to her that what happened to her was not insignificant, could be reported as an assault, and invited her to come to the station to make a statement. I would have said that to anyone for my whole career. But I also let her know that when she told me what happened, she sounded upset, and that it would have upset me too, scared me. I suggested that when something scary like that happens, it may have some residual effect. I let her know about free counselling options in the city if she needed someone to talk to about it.

A year ago I wouldn't have caught on to the significance of what happened to her. I wouldn't have taken the time to take the conversation beyond the usual nuts and bolts.

I'm trying to make sure I pay attention to my wins, my progress. But at the same time, physical symptoms and mental patterns keep popping up like a game of Whac-A-Mole. I've been reading *Radical Acceptance* by Tara Brach. In it she explains that a Buddhist method of dealing with challenging feelings is to imagine them as old friends, and welcome them to sit with you for a cup of tea. I try it, but I really don't like my old symptomatic friends. They are painfully annoying. Like that kid who rides back and forth on his bike in front of your house wanting to come in and play when you just want to be left alone. Like that person you recognize in the grocery store and immediately backtrack to a different aisle because you don't want to be cornered by them. Except I can't get away from these *friends*. They barge into my house and tail me in the grocery store demanding all of my attention.

I try to tell myself that it's okay. That it's unreasonable to have expected to sort everything out, to be symptom-free, to be healed after only four months. But after decades of fix, fix, fix, it's hard for me to be patient, to slowly unravel. I want to whack, whack, whack the moles into oblivion.

One day I get an email, which has been sent to all officers at the police station, from Family Services, a community-based organization which offers free counselling and programming. Their counsellors are offering a two-day workshop on trauma, with the goal of providing first responders with tools to address the impact of trauma. Two days in a group of people sounds like a recipe for severe dehydration from stress-sweating, but I want to find new tools to whack old moles, so I feel the fear and sign up anyway. In the meantime, I'm still practising Val's suggested strategies and other exercises I've read about. I'm not organized in what I do. I don't have a *plan of action,* a *practice.* I just sort of throw everything at the wall and see what sticks.

I also have my fourth meeting with Val. We talk about clothes.

"It is a complete waste of money and time." I shake my head in exasperation. "But I can't seem to stop it. And now I have three things coming up in the next few months, an in-service day of training at work, a two-day trauma session, and an awards ceremony, and all I can think of is 'what am I going to wear?' even though I *know* I have clothes I can already wear."

Val helps me explore my beliefs around clothing, how it helps me cope. She gives me suggestions for how to notice the urge to search and shop. Slow it down. Challenge my thinking. She talks about how she wasn't really happy with her outfit when she put it on today, but shrugged off the feeling. She does that sometimes, play-acts a little example of a healthy reaction to a situation. She suggests I might want to try wearing something out of my comfort zone. A colourful patterned shirt perhaps, a gaudy brooch. Something that would challenge my need to feel like I'm wearing clothes that are *just right,* to explore if I'm just as safe wearing something *not right.*

I nod and make a face suggesting I will consider it. I won't. Suggesting I wear something *not right* is like suggesting an astronaut try a spacewalk without a helmet. But still, I go home with the goal to buy nothing new for events coming up, to wear what I have.

Instead, I spend most of my spare time over the next few weeks online looking for the *just right* outfits that will keep me alive in the hostile atmosphere outside my house. I spend five hundred dollars and end up feeling ashamed and disgusted.

Other than the clothes, I feel fairly optimistic leading up to the trauma workshop. I feel like I'm going to be able to spend the two days without any physical symptoms. I feel optimistic because instead of dreading the event, like I usually do after

I make plans that sounded like a good idea at the time, I am looking forward to it.

The positive feeling stays with me until I start driving there. My chest and back muscles contract until they throb with pain, my heart ricochets around my ribcage, my neck and throat twist and convulse, and my clothes are soaked in sweat before I even park the car. I say my mantras. I try some somatic exercises. I try to welcome my symptomatic friends and sit with them for a while, but it doesn't work, so I try telling myself to stop being so ridiculous. That doesn't work either. But I feel the fear and walk into the room of twenty participants and three counsellors.

The workshop is held in a public meeting room on the main floor of the police station. Twenty chairs surround six large tables arranged in a U-shape. The three counsellors sit towards the front of the room near a screen for the PowerPoint.

Choosing a seat is tricky, but I settle on one at one of the back corners. After the counsellors welcome us and briefly outline what is to be expected, they invite us to take turns introducing ourselves. Waiting for my turn to introduce myself to a group of people is like being the disposable extra in the opening scene of the *Jaws* movie, except instead of being blissfully oblivious to my fate, I can see the shark fin approaching and know I will be helpless to stop the silvery killer from dragging me under the water. The closer it gets to my turn, the faster my heart beats. Most probably to the tempo of the *Jaws* theme song. I pray my deodorant is up to the challenge.

The group isn't what I expected. There are no firefighters, no paramedics, no other call-takers from other agencies. There is only one other police officer. The other participants are from Mobile Crisis, Animal Control, Saskatoon Search and Rescue, and Child Protective services. I'm surprised on two counts. First, that out of police, fire and ambulance, only two of us signed up. Out of police alone, that is only .04%. Is the other 99.96% of the force so okay that they don't have a need to learn about strategies to deal with trauma? I know what kinds of calls they go to. The things they see. The things I thank God I don't have to see. I hear the distress in officers' voices when they tell me about the fatal car accident in which a young woman was severed in half. The scene of a female so lost in a drug-induced psychosis that she clawed out her reproductive organs through her vagina. The male on meth who gouged out his own eyes with a spoon. Maybe no one else saw the email. Maybe everyone else has the help they need. I hope that's true.

I'm also surprised about the composition of the group, because I never considered Mobile Crisis, Animal Control, Saskatoon Search and Rescue, and Child Protective Services as first responder groups. But as they go around introducing themselves and explaining the challenges of their jobs, their presence here makes sense, and I start to feel like an imposter because I just answer the phone.

One of the first topics the counsellors introduce on the PowerPoint is a diagram of The Window of Tolerance, a concept developed by Dr. Dan Siegel. The diagram consists of two horizontal parallel lines. The space in between the lines represents the Window of Tolerance, wherein the body and mind are able to self-regulate. The space above the line represents the hyper-aroused state, which has a long list of symptoms, including anxiety, sleeplessness, panic and chronic pain.

The space below the line represents the hypo-aroused state, with another long list of symptoms, including disorientation, depression, and dissociation. There are two lines on the chart. A wavy grey line runs between the two lines signifying the natural rise and fall of a person's nervous response within the Window of Tolerance. A red line, stemming from a traumatic event, runs in a jagged up-and-down motion between hyper-arousal and hypo-arousal interspersed with plateaus on both ends signifying being either stuck "on" in hyper-arousal and stuck "off" in hypo-arousal.

I stare at the image, read the symptoms and notice two things. I notice that at this moment, I have many of the symptoms described in the hyper-arousal stage, but I also feel some of the symptoms in the hypo-arousal state. I wonder if that's even possible, if I might be misinterpreting what is going on inside me. But if I am experiencing symptoms of both states it might explain why sometimes I feel frozen on the outside but revved up on the inside. Like a cold and hot weather front have collided in me and created a storm that churns in my body but has no release.

I also notice the pattern of the red line: the spiky ups and downs, the stuck on and off. I look at the symptoms again. It looks suspiciously similar to my bipolar symptoms and cycles. I always thought I was diagnosed with too little scrutiny, though I never thought to get a second opinion. Even though my cycles and symptoms seemed to follow the bipolar pattern, I often questioned if I was actually bipolar. I knew something was "off" about my moods and behaviour. I didn't think my apprehension about walking across a bridge or driving a car because I worried a suicidal impulse might spur me to throw myself onto the rocks or drive into oncoming traffic was normal. But every time I questioned the diagnosis, I went back, looked at the markers for bipolar disorder and they seemed to fit. But now, looking at this graph, I'm not so sure. Looking at the graph, I'm inclined to think that my diagnosis might have been wrong.

The counsellors are finished with the graph and move on. The material they cover is diverse and interesting. They welcome participation, which makes me nervous because somehow, I can't stop myself from participating. It's something I've recognized for years. If a teacher or professor asks a question and no one answers right away, I feel like I am expected to fill the void, contribute, that something bad will happen if I don't.

But it's not just in a classroom environment. It's in most social environments. I feel like the spotlight is on me and I'm expected to perform. And I do. I try to answer the question. I try to be funny. I try to be smart. I try to have a good story, a clever quip. I overshare. I make an ass of myself at parties and on the dance floor. I say and do things that wake me up at three in the morning, dripping in sweat, with the python wrapped around my chest.

I have a co-worker who has an uncanny ability to fly under the radar. She glides in and out of work quietly, her voice never rises above a low murmur. She somehow orbits around the workplace gossip, never getting sucked into the black hole of drama. She attends our training days and can go the whole day without raising her hand to ask a question, make a comment or observation. Some days I forget she's there. Other days I watch her closely, enviously, trying to figure out her secret. But I never have, and in the trauma workshop, as expected, I start a pattern of raising my hand, contributing, oversharing, every act spiralling me further in the hyper-arousal zone.

The counsellors ask the following question: "What were you like before?" They look around the room for a response. As usual, I think they are expecting me to respond, but I am truly stumped by the question. What was I like before? Before what? I marinate in the question for a while, and then it hits me. They want to know what I was like before the traumatic event.

And then something else hits me: the reason I never recognized the signs of trauma in myself, even though I had been educated in the workplace on it numerous times over the last ten years. Every time someone did a presentation on trauma, it focused on learning to recognize the signs of a change in feelings and behaviour *after* an event. But I never realized there was a traumatic event, and I think the signs and symptoms of trauma were so gradual and happened so early in my life that I didn't even notice a change. At least not a clearly defined change. I can't pin down what I was like before. But I recall two memories that suggest I realized something was going on.

Both memories are from shop class. In the first incident, the teacher was trying to explain to me something about sanding a chisel I had made. I remember him standing in front of me talking, but I wasn't there. My body was there, but the rest of me was somewhere else. I wasn't daydreaming and I didn't have other thoughts on my mind. It was like my consciousness was outside of my body. I remember fighting with myself to focus on what he was saying, but I couldn't bring myself back into my body. It was like being drunk and trying to stop the room from spinning. I remember thinking *this isn't me.*

The other incident happened when we were learning how to put rivets onto our toolbox. I'd put the rivets in, as instructed, but something wasn't right. I couldn't figure it out. I showed the teacher, who said he'd never seen that before. I should have used the rivets to fasten two pieces of metal together, but I had put them in a single metal piece. The effect was like needing to staple two pieces of paper together but only putting the staple in one sheet.

Now to be fair, I don't need to be traumatized to not understand something, have a lack of concentration or make a mistake. Just the other night, at dinner, my son, Max, was talking about a common saying and wondering about the origins. Jeff and Maddie joined in the discussion. I was confused. "I've never heard this saying before."

They all looked at me in astonishment.

"You've *never* heard it?" Maddie and Jeff said at once.

"How could you have never heard it before?" Maddie leaned forward, a look of pure incredulity on her face.

"I don't know," I said. Where did *you* hear it?"

"Everyone knows it!" Maddie threw her hands up in the air. I shrugged.

"Wait a minute," said Max, "what do *you* think I said?"

"Thumb the horse's mouth."

They burst into laughter.

"*From* the horse's mouth, not *thumb*," they howled.

I began to laugh too.

Incidents like these are not uncommon with me, but when they happen, they generally don't stick in my mind the same way that the two incidents in class did. Whenever I recall the metal shop incidents, and they have come to mind frequently over the decades, I also recall the feeling I had, the feeling that something was wrong with me. The reason I couldn't concentrate on something wasn't because of a misunderstanding, or being preoccupied, it was because I just wasn't there. So where was I? On the lookout for the boy's roving hands, shark-like smile, and irritating laugh.

As the counsellors discuss the reason for asking "What were you like before?" I start to wonder, if there was a "before" me and an "after" me, had anyone noticed the difference? I was fourteen at the time, still growing, brain still developing, so if I was changing in those ways, would any other change even be noticeable, or just chalked up to typical awkward teenage years?

I think about a cat Jeff and I used to have. A nervous tabby tortoise cross named Dir Dir. One day, while I was brushing my teeth in the bathroom, she came racing in to jump onto the sink to drink from the faucet. In order to get to the sink, she used the toilet as a stepping stool, but on this occasion the toilet seat was up and she plunged into the water. She propelled herself out in an instant, leaving me doubled over in laughter as she ran into the hallway. I peeked out into the hallway and caught her licking away at her wet fur, but as soon as she saw me, she immediately stopped and assumed a far-off gaze, as if to give the impression she was too engrossed in thinking about something deeply philosophical to notice me staring at her toilet-drenched fur. She then turned her placid gaze to inquire why I was laughing and looking at her because nothing had happened. I ducked my head back into the bathroom and slowly peeked around the corner, and caught her grooming herself again, but when she saw me looking, she again assumed her *nothing to see here* posture. I kept ducking and peeking, and she constantly stopped licking and kept pretending there was nothing to see.

I've frequently thought about Dir Dir and the toilet incident. Mostly because it makes me laugh, but also because I always felt I somehow knew what was going on in her head, something I identified with. Now I think I know what it might be. At first, I thought it may have been an issue of pride, but I don't think cats register the feeling of humiliation. Instead, I think it is an issue of self-preservation. Dir Dir may have been trying to gloss over her moment of weakness. I think I relate to Dir Dir in that moment because I'm starting to suspect that all of these years, I've been doing what she was doing: trying to act normal, hoping no one sees me drenched in toilet water, licking it away when no one is looking. I've been trying to hide my weakness. And because I've been trying to act normal, and because I never told anyone what happened, then how could my parents, friends, or anyone who knew me *before* have noticed a change? Because I think I was very good at looking normal, looking like a well-adjusted teenager. If anyone were to play a game of *spot the traumatized teenager in the high school yearbooks,* I don't think they'd point at all the photos of me participating in social activities and smiling.

What was I like before? The question haunts me as the workshop continues. I try to think back. All I get is a blank. I only had fourteen years of before, there are over thirty years of after. Then the question morphs into: What would I have been like if it never happened? A rush of dark dismay passes through me and grips my heart.

I have smart kids. I have sometimes found them sitting at the dining table engrossed in a conversation about math. I never knew math could be a topic of conversation beyond the evil necessity of it. Jeff and I don't take credit for their smarts. We suspect it may be a double case of switched at birth, that there's a married couple with high IQs out there wondering what happened to their kids. Maddie and Max are smart, but I often think about all the little accidents. The times I accidentally hit their heads on the side of the car while putting them in their car seats. The times I carried them on my hip and had a lapse in my spatial awareness and caught their heads on a door jamb. The times they ran head first straight into the dining room table, a monkey bar, the slide. I think about it and wonder how many IQ points did each little event shave off? How much smarter could they have been?

Now I'm wondering the same thing about myself. How much did each encounter with the boy shave off the original me? How much is left? How much was replaced by coping and symptoms of hypo- and hyper-arousal? How much more focused could I have been in school if I hadn't been so vigilant and disconnected? What different life choices would I have made? What friends would I have kept? I start to go down a rabbit hole of what-ifs and possible parallel universes where that original Karin, that Karin prime could exist. But I stop myself.

I stop myself because all of those universes would have probably put me on a path that wouldn't have intersected with a tall, blond, blue-eyed Saskatchewan guy with great shoulders. They wouldn't have included Maddie and Max. The thought of no Jeff, no Maddie, and no Max is exponentially, devastatingly worse than any regret or mourning of *what-ifs* or *could-have-beens*. I can't change the past, and even if I could, I wouldn't. I couldn't take that risk.

Even if I were assured that I would still end up with Jeff and the kids in my Karin prime parallel universe, it doesn't mean that my life would have been better, because every decision in that universe would put me on a course where I might encounter different life challenges, different traumas.

Shortly after my first meeting with Val, one part of me asked, *Why me?* I pondered the question for about thirty seconds, before another part of me answered, *Why not me?* Why should I have been the one singularly fortunate person on the planet to glide through life without adversity? The idea of trying to get through life without encountering problems, even trauma, is unrealistic. I was bound to meet up with it somewhere. So, the problem isn't so much the boy in the shop class. The problem may be more that it happened in the early 1980s, when there wasn't clear education or language about sexual assault or trauma. That even if someone believed what was happening was wrong, stopped it, noticed the changes in me and tried to help, there may not have been the kind of help, the kind of strategies, the kind of support there is today. I can't ever know how "Karin Prime" might have turned out. But I would bet she would have had problems and challenges to work out. She could have still benefitted from a Val. I can't change the past, but I can do my best to reclaim what's left and rebuild what I can.

I make it through both days of the workshop. We watch a Ted Talk. We explore boundaries. We are each given a large piece of paper on which to draw a tree of life and fill in the roots, trunk, and branches with words and phrases related to various themes. We get a visit from an emotional support dog. We practise breathing exercises, visualization and progressive muscle relaxation. We learn about the Pennebaker expressive writing protocol. I fill pages of the notebook I brought with me with quotes about trauma, websites to check out, and therapeutic approaches to explore.

I hightail it out of the workshop when it is over and spend the next four days using the Pennebaker expressive writing protocol to help me decompress after being outside my Window of Tolerance for two days. I end each writing session with one minute of gratitude journaling, which the counsellors also recommended. I make a plan to keep a gratitude journal for a month, just to see if it helps. I review my journal and my new tools, and prepare myself to whack more moles.

11

always thought I had a healthy attitude towards sex because I believed it was a natural part of being a human and didn't think it was wrong or dirty. I believe people when they say sex can be a very positive, feel-good experience; I just never felt like that was the case for me, because I don't feel very *sexual* myself. I don't feel particularly feminine. I have a fairly platonic relationship with my sex parts. My breasts and buttocks don't get lotion. I don't own pretty underwear. It's not that I'm averse to my breasts and my genitals. I can look at them and touch them, but I've always felt that I wouldn't miss them if they were gone, that I'd be relieved to wake up and find they'd left a note: *Dear Karin, This relationship isn't really working out, we've met someone who really appreciates us and have decided to move on. No hard feelings, Right Breast, Left Breast, Vagina et al.*

Even though I feel this way, I accept that sex should be a healthy part of life, a healthy part of a marriage. I know Jeff likes to have sex and I don't want to deprive him of it, and I do like being close to him. I remember once grilling my friend Mirjana about how often she and her husband had sex, but she wouldn't give me a direct answer, so I did an internet search on how many times a week a couple should have sex in order to have a normal sex life. I couldn't find anything definitive, so I came up with a general rule of almost every other day, at the very least two times a week, with a week off for my menstrual cycle.

It's not that sex hurts or feels bad physically, it's just it's hard for me to feel anything. Having any part of my body touched is about as sensuous and pleasurable as having someone rubbing my fingernail. I just don't register it. I can have an orgasm, but it's more about releasing tension than enjoying the experience. It's about as satisfying as a sneeze. Glad *that's* over. And when it's over, I feel used, resentful because I don't get as much out of it as my partner.

I see how sex is celebrated in books, magazines, movies and TV but I just don't connect with what is represented. I don't get what they are talking about, what the big deal is. To me, sex is about duty and expediency, not enjoyment and fulfilment.

So yeah, that was what I thought was a healthy attitude towards sex. But I've been rethinking it lately.

I talk to Val about it in our next session, a few weeks after the trauma workshop. She asks if my interaction with the boy in ninth-grade shop class was my first sexual experience. I answer yes. I'd kissed a boy once in the sixth grade, but no one had ever touched my private parts.

Val holds out her hands explaining that my first sexual experience (one hand) and violence (the other hand) were fused into one experience. She presses her hands together to demonstrate (double whammy). She then asks what my sexual experiences were like after.

"I was like a heat-seeking missile with boys." I look up at the ceiling, shaking my head. "It's like I had this energy that could only be dissipated by getting a boyfriend, making out with him a few times and then breaking up with him. It seemed to be a three-month cycle but not always. I didn't have sex until I was eighteen."

"And how was that?" Val tilts her head to the side and smiles gently. "In a healthy relationship there is time for experimentation. Finding out what you like, what kinds of touches feel good, exploring, curiosity."

I shake my head. "Nope, it was zero to sixty, kissing, then straight to sex."

And that is what it was like through college. Zero in on a guy, initiate a sexual relationship almost immediately, then break up. Still a three-month cycle, sometimes shorter, much shorter, sometimes longer. At the time I told myself I was a liberated woman who wasn't constrained by societal expectations of feminine purity.

But that rationalization didn't fit. I wasn't having sex because I felt I had full agency over my body, because I enjoyed it. I was having sex because I felt compelled. It wasn't until later in my married life that I recognized it was even a pattern, a pattern I looked back on with deep regret and shame, with contempt for past Karin. But even though I recognized it, I didn't understand why I did it, until I read about trauma and learned about repetition compulsion.

Repetition compulsion is an unconscious attempt to re-enact a traumatic event in order to overcome or master it. It may explain why a person who grew up in an abusive household chooses an abusive partner or why people who experience sexual abuse as children are more likely to become sex workers.

While my throwing myself at boys and men seems like a counter-intuitive reaction to being repeatedly sexually assaulted in the ninth grade, when I read about repetition compulsion something clicked into place, and I finally started to understand what was going on with me.

It goes something like this. What I learned in ninth-grade shop class was that my body did not belong to me. Anyone could have access to my body at any time. My "no" did not matter. My "stop" didn't make a difference, and so a part of me was constantly on guard for when it would happen next. And if I remember correctly, my pattern didn't start to ramp up until the summer after ninth grade ended.

When I was still attending the class, I knew when it was going to happen. There was some regularity. My body was waiting for it. It happened, then it was over. I could get on with my day.

Afterwards, I didn't know where the next assault was going to come from. But my body had learned that it *was* going to come, so it would stay on high alert, in a state of constant vigilance. If I sought out a boy, or later a man, with whom I initiated kissing, touching and then later sex, then I controlled the experience. I could control who I let "attack" me and when, and after I allowed it to happen my body would say, *Ah, here's what I've been expecting and now that it's over, I can relax.* But because my body was used to it on such a regular basis, the relaxing never lasted, thus the reason for the cycle.

With my vast experience—consisting of six meetings with Val, and reading a few books on trauma—I can't say that this is a psychologically sound theory. I understand the mind is a complicated beast and that my motivations, observations, and rationalizations may be more self-serving than objective, and I'm sure mental health professionals may have other explanations. All I *can* say with certainty is that this explanation seems to fit. It makes sense. It releases some of the shame, lets in some self-love, and even gratitude and respect for my body and mind for trying to keep me safe as best as it could. Some days making sense is enough.

I look back on those years and I consider myself lucky, extremely lucky. For some reason, not related to intelligence, planning, or intention, I ended up with nice guys, safe guys. None of those boys and men were mentally, physically or sexually abusive at all, ever. They would never have had a clue about my reason for throwing myself at them. By all appearances, I was an enthusiastic instigator.

I remember one high school party in particular. It was at a house with woods behind it. I was chatting with a boy a few years older than myself, which always seemed like a compliment in high school, and he asked me if I wanted to go for a walk in the woods. I said no. He seemed nice. He smiled. He was cute, but his offer felt like danger. He immediately lost interest in our conversation and walked away.

I've thought about that moment a lot over the years because I remember it as being a time when my intuition kept me safe. And it makes me think it's kept me safe all along. But I can't take credit for my intuition. It is all subconscious. I have friends and family members who have toxic, dangerous partners and friends, and I used to blame them for staying in those relationships. But now I'm starting to see how those relationships, and people, might be part of something more complicated. Just as I ended up with safe people subconsciously, they may have ended up with *unsafe* people for similar reasons.

But accepting this theory of re-enacting trauma comes with a flip side. Because if I claim the reasoning for my previous unexplainable behaviour, then I also have to consider it as a reason for the behaviour of others. I have to consider it for the boy: the teenage boy with feathered brown hair and a charming smile. The boy who, for some reason, grabbed and humiliated me regularly in class and sometimes in the hallway. I think about how what he did seems like a cycle too, a compulsion. And I ask myself whether he might have been re-enacting his own traumatic experience. And if that was the case, if he was just a teenage boy dealing with unresolved trauma and acting it out, if that was his coping, if that was keeping him safe, then I have to be willing to have some compassion for him, some understanding. After all, he was just a kid too.

I've been hoping the combination of my sessions with Val, my journaling, and the therapeutic exercises I've been doing would be enough to reshape my thoughts about sex. Perhaps if I understood what shaped my feelings about sex, not only could I fulfil my self-imposed sexual obligations without further scrutiny, but the sex would magically bloom into a joyful and ecstatic experience that makes me feel like one with Jeff and the universe. But that has not been the case. Val gave me some suggestions: explore safe touch, take turns giving and receiving, notice neutral and safe experiences. I've tried those, but I need more. I need a program, a method, a line of attack. I need a book.

I buy *The Sexual Healing Journey, A Guide for Survivors of Sexual Abuse* by Wendy Maltz. Towards the beginning of the book Maltz lists the Top Ten Sexual Symptoms of Sexual Abuse. I check off nine of them. I don't have a perfect score because the tenth symptom requires having a penis, which I do not have.

To be fair, that is my historical score. Two of the symptoms no longer apply. So really my current score is seven. Seventy percent. A solid C.

Also included in the book is a Sexual Effects Inventory consisting of 144 statements divided into six categories. I check off fifty of the statements and put question marks next to three of them, because I'm not sure they apply. But the other fifty feel true, so thirty-four percent. A failing grade.

Some of the statements I check off are beliefs that, while true, come as a surprise even though I immediately recognize them, but the majority are beliefs that have previously crossed my mind, but never crystallized into coherent thoughts. I sigh and my shoulders droop a little more every time I check off another statement. I didn't realize how much I had been affected, how deep it went, and it shocks me how the actions of a teenage boy over three decades ago dictate how I respond to sex as a middle-aged woman. But while the assessment is sobering, I keep in mind that I didn't check off everything, that I don't have every sexual problem known to humankind.

The book talks about what actual healthy attitudes towards sex are, using words like *healing energy, communication* and *empowerment.*

They all seem like foreign concepts to me, and I'm a little skeptical that anyone really feels that way about sex. Surely the people who check off those boxes are about as common as unicorns. But being a sexual unicorn sounds nice, and I'd like to see if I can become one. Before I try, though, I feel like I need to try something Maltz suggests: a healing vacation from sex. I want to take it in hopes of hitting the reset button on how I view sex.

However, Jeff would also have to go on the same vacation, and I don't know how I am going to talk to him about it.

It's not the first time I've had to ask something difficult of Jeff that relates to our intimacy. Last spring, when he was sick with a cold, I slept in the spare bedroom so I wouldn't catch it. I noticed I slept much better. Part of it is because I wake up easily to most sounds and movements. The other part is, because I am a shift worker, I sometimes don't turn around all that well and wake up in the middle of the night unable to go back to sleep. When I do, I'm worried about waking Jeff with my tossing and turning, going to get a snack, padding to the living room to read. That worry further inhibits my ability to relax and fall back asleep. When I slept in the spare room, I felt less anxious waking in the middle of the night, and found I got to sleep sooner by staying in bed and reading. And because I am a shift worker, sleeping well is a highly prized commodity. So, I asked Jeff what he thought about me having my own bedroom. He took it a little hard, he was a little hurt, but he understood. He gave way and now I have my own room.

Then in December, when I started connecting my physical and mental reactions in some situations to unresolved trauma, I asked more of Jeff. He likes to come up behind me, wrap his arms around me, give me a kiss on the neck. Why wouldn't he? It's a classic scene in movies and on TV. It's what lovers do. But when I'm washing dishes or cutting up vegetables and Jeff comes into the kitchen, I feel like I'm in a horror movie and the ominous music has started. I go on high alert, bracing myself in anticipation, knowing it's only a matter of time until he wraps his arms around me. When he does, my insides try to jump out of my skin, acting like I've just faced off with an axe murderer instead of my best friend, the love of my life. And it makes me feel despicable—what kind of person wouldn't want their partner to show them love and affection in this way? But in my new reality, my reaction makes sense.

I asked Jeff to stop. I explained why. He agreed, and he did. And it helps.

Jeff is very affectionate and appreciative with his words. He comments often on how beautiful and sexy he thinks I am. He enjoys suggestive banter. He can turn pulling hair out of the drain into clever sexual innuendo. He's cute. He's funny. He's playful. What kind of wife wouldn't appreciate that her husband of twenty-five years still wants to have sexy wordplay with her?

This wife. So, I asked him to stop, but I didn't explain why. I didn't explain that instead of being the fun verbal exchange I know he means it to be, I take it as what I imagine to be one of his never-ending ploys to try and get me to have sex. I take it as pressure. Again, he agreed and stopped. It helps, but it's not enough, and now I have an even bigger ask.

I write down some thoughts in a letter. When I reach my limit, when pretending and performing while having sex becomes too much, when I know something better is out there, when I finally have the courage, I invite him to sit down for a discussion, at the end of March. Why let the month go out like a lamb? Jeff agrees and we sit cross-legged on the twin bed in my room while I read him this letter.

"I've been scared to talk to you about what I am about to say because I have been afraid that you are going to reject me. I thought I could work through my sexual issues and still try to fulfil your sexual needs, but it's not working. I need some time off from sex. I need to know that you love and value me even when there is no expectation of having sex with me. I need to know that when you spend time with me, hug me, hold my hand, massage me, sit next to me, cuddle me, kiss me, that your endgame is not to seduce me, or try to have sex. The only way I can know this, really know this, is to experience it."

I then explain about the book. Tell him how many statements I checked off. Explain what a vacation from sex is, and how I think it might be helpful. All the while Jeff deflates, withdraws, and shrinks back from me.

"What is sex for you?" I ask, expecting a simple answer like "It feels good."

Instead, he ponders the question, gathers his thoughts and begins. He starts out exactly how I expect. By saying that on the physical level it feels good. But then he starts to talk about the other levels it feels good on: spiritual and emotional. He uses phrases like "intense communication", "emotional connection" and "validation of our love" and words like sharing, safety, trust, and joy.

As he talks, I stare at him, dumbfounded. The things he is describing all fall squarely in the category of healthy sexual attitudes. He checks off all of the boxes—A plus—and I realize, either I'm married to a unicorn, or a healthy sexual attitude isn't that uncommon or out of reach.

I have two reactions. One, that I want what he has. I want to be a unicorn with him. And the second reaction is deep guilt that I'm denying this fantastic experience to the man I love most, my best friend.

I lean towards him. "I want what you have," I say.

"I want that for you too," he replies earnestly, frustrated.

"I know," I say, "but I think I really need this break. I need to know that you love me without having sex with me."

"I do!"

"I know." I point to my head. "But I just really need to know." I place my hand over my heart.

I tell him I don't feel this way because of anything he's done or not done, that the damage happened before I even met him, that it's not his fault, that, according to the book, he's a secondary victim.

He agrees to the vacation—what else is he going to do? He doesn't say much else, that day or the next, about anything. For two days we avoid each other as much as we can in our little house. Me because I'm trying to give him space, him because he has a hard time looking at me. I can't tell if he's hurt, angry or both. I begin to get a sinking feeling in the pit of my stomach while I wait for him to come to some sort of decision he seems to be making. I prepare myself for him to break the news to me that this is the last straw. That he's endured enough of my moods, my cycles, my fixing, my shopping, my demands. That the one good thing left about me was sex, and without it I'm not worth the trouble.

I play over scenarios in my mind. Will he leave or will he ask me to leave? Who will get the house? What will happen to the kids? Will they still love me, knowing I ruined the marriage? Part of me thinks I should move back home for a while, stay with my parents until, I don't know, until I stop being so broken. The other part wants to stay with our children, but maybe they'd be better off without me too. The thoughts circle around my head while Jeff and I silently circle around each other.

Finally, Jeff asks me if we can talk. He doesn't smile reassuringly. He takes a few deep breaths, trying to find the best way to break it to me. I brace myself in an attempt to prepare to hear his decision, accept that I deserve it. "I've been thinking about what we talked about the other day." He presses his lips into a grim line.

My heart races and my jaw clenches. I hold my breath. I'm not prepared for this yet.

He looks directly at me with his serious sky-blue eyes that used to love me. "And I want you to know…"

Oh God. I think. *I'm not ready, I'm not ready, I'm not ready.*

"I want you to know." He places his hands on my shoulders, holding me together, looking into my eyes. "That your 'no' is better than anyone else's 'yes.'"

I choke back a breath. I'm not sure I heard him right.

"Your no…" He focuses his blue eyes intently on mine, trying to laser beam the meaning of his words past my defences. "…is better than anyone else's yes."

And this time his words sink in to my forehead, and they are so heavy with meaning they fall to my heart, crack it open and plunge in.

With the shell surrounding my heart broken, his every "I love you" from the past twenty-five years finally enters, like little balls of light that spread and warm my chest, torso, my limbs and face. And I finally understand the sincerity of those words, I finally believe them. I finally know how it feels to feel his love.

I tell Val about it a few weeks later.

"That's huge." Her eyes go wide as her eyebrows raise.

"Yeah." I nod. "That's huge."

Jeff and I take a vacation from sex, but we don't take a vacation from each other. We watch one of Wendy Maltz's videos on

YouTube. The video is dated, the participants are brave. It describes and demonstrates simple exercises for couples to practise, exercises like writing on each other's backs and hand clapping.

We try them, feeling a little silly. They help. We take things slow. And slowly things begin to shift. I notice my arms first. A strange tingling sensation runs through them as we do a simple, non-sexual touching exercise. It feels as though my arms have been asleep for decades and are starting to wake up, but instead of the pins and needles sensation, I feel something else. I feel pleasure. And it's a pleasure that shoots up my arms when I caress Jeff's arms, his chest. And the sensation is almost overwhelming, but I can't get enough of it and I take it as a sign I'm starting to heal, and I'm starting to understand why sex is such a big deal.

I don't know if the feeling will stay, if it will spread. I don't know if I will ever become a unicorn. But things are starting to get a little bit better, and a little bit better is good enough for now.

12

On the morning of May 8th, I sip my coffee and stare out the kitchen window facing the backyard. The fat white jackrabbit from winter has turned lean and brown and is lounging in the yard under a cherry tree heavy with buds. Rosie crouches on the deck staring at the rabbit while a trio of magpies perched on the fence shriek at her until she finally creeps towards the back door and gives me a woebegone look. I go to the door and let her back in.

"Are those birds giving you a hard time?"

Rosie gives a bellyaching *mew* and makes a beeline to the front door, where I let her out as quietly as I can so as to outsmart the magpies. She takes a quick scan of the skies, then slinks along the house and fence line, staying out of the open as best she can.

I go back to the kitchen to find something for breakfast from the fridge, where I am stopped in my tracks by the magnetic calendar and the words written on today's date: Awards Banquet.

It is the day of the Saskatoon Police Exemplary Service Awards banquet, where I am to receive The Superintendent's Award of Commendation for work I did on a missing person call that turned into a murder investigation. It was one of the calls that I had initially wanted to talk about with Val last November, when instead our conversation was hijacked by my *life event*.

The banquet has been hanging over my head for two months. I've tried not to think about it, but waves of dread wash over me regularly when it comes to mind.

Val suggested that I have choices, but my co-worker Jill nominated me for the award. My other co-worker Char, who is on the awards committee, backed the nomination. My team then bought tickets to come and support me for my big night. It's an honour to receive it and I feel it would be ungrateful not to go. Plus, I want to want to go. I want to be able to dress up, spend an evening with my family and co-workers, eat an average buffet meal, listen to well-intentioned but slightly boring and overlong speeches, walk up onto the stage for my thirty seconds of fame and a picture with my superintendent, and not have it be a *thing*. Not have the whole night, the whole two months previous, feel like I am on a plane waiting to skydive with a parachute I'm pretty sure doesn't work.

I tried to journal about it, telling myself that it's not such a big deal, that lots of people are getting awards, and no one will really be paying attention to me. I will be just a blip on their radar. I say my mantras—*They are not them, now is not then.* Every day I read the *Personal Bill of Rights* Val suggested I look up online. And there were moments I thought it was going to be okay. But today I'm hoping that the stomach pains I'm feeling are an appendix about to burst, and I walk to the drugstore because I'm too scared to drive for fear I will subconsciously get into an accident bad enough to land me in the hospital, which would be okay except for the fact that I don't want anyone else to get hurt, and we can't afford to have the car damaged. On my way, I see a woman walking a large dog and wish that it would break free from the leash, attack me and maim me just enough that I'll have an excuse not to go.

But on the bright side, my thoughts aren't suicidal, so that's a win. I'm still able to resist the impulse to change my hair. And while I did spend a ton of time walking through stores and looking online, I didn't buy anything new, and will be wearing what I already have, the whole outfit. I'm counting that as a win too.

I pace around the house the whole day, unable to lasso my mind into any kind of focus, until it's finally time to get dressed in my black skirt, black sleeveless tunic, and black cardigan. I don't wear any jewellery because I don't think it's appropriate. Other officers are getting awards for heroic acts: lifting a car off a man until the paramedics arrive, extinguishing the flames on a man who set himself on fire, pulling a woman out of the river. I didn't help anyone, no one was saved. A woman was murdered, a man is in jail, and the families of each are left to suffer the fallout.

I could have worn my police dress tunic and saved myself the hassle of the question of what to wear. But every time I considered it, I immediately got caught in an undertow. A dress tunic has too many parts to it: gloves, lanyard, hat. My tunic dress pants no longer fit, so I would have needed to get new ones, and to have them hemmed. Plus, the whole outfit is a furnace, and I don't want to sweat any more than I already will.

Outfit on, hair and makeup done, I walk into the kitchen, where Jeff and Maddie are waiting for me. Max couldn't come because he is at work.

"Hey Mom, are you excited about your big night?"

I burst into tears.

I tell Val about it in our next meeting. She swivels to her desk, picks up a marker and walks over to the whiteboard on her door, where she draws a triangle.

I fall back against the couch and roll my eyes. *I hate the triangle.* We've done it a few times before, and it always starts with her saying the same thing.

"Okay, what are your thoughts when you are anticipating an event like the banquet?"

I answer the way I always answer.

"I don't have any thoughts. I just think about the event and then my body starts betraying me."

And Val always responds the same way while looking at me, so I have to mentally roll my eyes so she doesn't see what a bad client I am.

"Thoughts, Feelings, and Behaviours"—Val points at a corner for each word—"are all inter-connected, which means, if you are having a feeling"—she points at the feeling corner—"there is likely a thought behind it." She points at the thought corner: "And for thoughts, there is usually a behaviour." She points at the Behaviour corner. "So, what are some of the thoughts you are having when your body is betraying you?"

Ugh, she just doesn't get it. I don't have any thoughts, so why do we have to talk about them? Why can't she just give me a formula for stopping my heart from jumping out of my chest, and my sweat glands from ruining my clothes?

Val stands firmly pointing the marker at the "Thought" corner, waiting for my answer.

"Well, I guess I'm thinking that I just don't want to go."

Val nods and writes it down in the thought corner and also scrawls *avoidance* in the "Behaviour" corner.

"I'm scared everyone is going to be looking at me."

She writes that down, too, and adds *fear* to the "Feeling" corner.

"I never know what to wear. I don't know what I'm going to say."

The list grows as she writes.

"I mean, it just feels like so much effort, but I usually push through and go to stuff but then feel worse after."

She puts, *pushes through* in the "Behaviour" corner and *frustration and feeling worse* in the "Feeling" corner.

"I did feel better after I cried."

I remember collapsing onto Jeff's shoulder, soaking his shirt with my tears.

"It released a lot of the tension I'd been feeling. And the night turned out okay. I mean, my clothes were drenched in sweat, and my heart just pounded all night, but I made it through. I mean, of course I made it through. I always make it through. But I'm tired of just making it through. I'm tired of enduring, grinning and bearing it, feeling the fear and doing it anyway. I'm not asking to never be nervous, feel a little awkward, or a little unsure or uncomfortable. I just want to be able to leave the house, go to the store, a party, dinner with friends, and not feel like this.

"I mean, just the other day I went for a walk, and saw a table on the corner with two little girls selling lemonade. Right away I got nervous about passing them, wondering what I should do. I mean, I know what I want to do. I want to turn around and take a different street, so I don't feel like I have to interact with them. But that is beyond ridiculous. I'm an adult. I shouldn't be afraid of a possible social interaction with two girls. I shouldn't have to change my walking path to avoid them. But what do I do if I do walk by? Should I talk to them? Should I buy some lemonade just to be a nice person? But I don't want any lemonade. So, do I ignore them? What if they talk to *me*? What if they ask me if I want lemonade? What kind of person doesn't buy lemonade from two little kids? How do I say no to them?"

Val sits back in her chair, then swivels to her bookshelf, pulls out a book, rolls over to the couch, opens it up and places it next to me.

The pages are filled with questions. It's some type of assessment. After I answer them all, Val does a tally. While she may have enough experience to make a diagnosis, she doesn't have the academic qualifications to make one. But she does explain what I may be experiencing.

"It seems that your baseline anxiety level may be above normal." She motions with her hand slightly above her head to signify a high level.

"What might be helpful is to try to bring down your level of anxiety, and find out what your normal would feel like, your baseline. And to do that I have three suggestions you can choose from. The first one, to try a month of focused Cognitive Behavioural Therapy, where you examine your thoughts, feelings and behaviours. It requires a time commitment, because you will be doing it for everything that has this effect on you."

She means the triangle. Ugh, no thank you.

"Another option, take a full month off of any type of commitments. Don't schedule anything that you can't cancel, and add some cardio to your daily routine to work off some of the energy."

Not going to anything or being around anyone for a month? I like that idea very much.

"And the third option, talk to your family doctor about medication. Some people find it helpful, because after one to two weeks on the medication, they start to regulate and then realize what a more normalized baseline feels like. It helps them determine how much of a difference there is between up here"—she holds her hand up to forehead level to represent a higher level of anxiety—"and here." She lowers her hand to chest level to represent a normal level.

The medication is tempting. I am curious to know what a more normal response to, say, grocery shopping, would be. I'd like to know what the normal is without having to change anything, but I don't like taking medication.

"I think I'll take option two. The cardio and no commitments."

Val nods and makes a note of it.

I go home and tell Jeff my plan not to make plans for a month. I tell him July is going to be the Month of Karin. My summer holidays are scheduled for that month and we have only one social commitment on the calendar, which I give myself permission to cancel at any time.

I start to look forward to it. Knowing I have a month in which I would schedule nothing I couldn't cancel feels liberating. Like I can put my guard down, not have to mentally prepare for some unknown event.

It's not as if my life is filled with events: it's not. I don't have much of a social life. The biggest commitment I have right now, other than work, is lawn bowling, which occurs twice a week with extremely kind people. It's a perfect way to spend an evening. A nice walk to the park, bowl a game, have tea, cookies, a visit and walk home. It's not too strenuous, and it's a nice break from our usual after-dinner TV watching. But even that commitment feels like a weight on my shoulders. I should be able to go lawn bowling without it being a thing. But just knowing I should be able to go without having a reaction doesn't change the fact that I do, and so for the month of July lawn bowling is off the table.

With my calendar clear, I start off the month looking forward to discovering what my normal will feel like, but immediately run into a snag. The first day. Before I get out of bed.

All of my life, I've been a sleeper. My mom blames herself because I was the fourth child, and she was content to let me sleep, because as long as I was sleeping that meant one less kid to deal with. And who in their right mind could blame her? Certainly not me. But I also don't think that's the reason I'm a sleeper. I think it's just my nature. I've never been a real go-getter, someone that needs to get up at the crack of dawn to get busy. My natural pace is a bit slower. I like to ease into my days. But even though I've always liked to sleep in, I don't always remember dreading the day once I woke up.

I'm not sure when it happened, but going by the recent theme in my life, if I had to take a guess, it would be sometime during or after ninth grade. Before that, while I liked to sleep in, I didn't have an issue getting out of bed once I'd woken up. But after, getting out of bed was hard. The only thing that bypassed that difficulty was if I had to get out of bed to go to do something I had to do: like work or take care of the kids when they were little. But a day off, that's a whole different story.

So, in July, the Month of Karin, my first day off, I'm lying in bed noticing how I feel. I should feel free, unhindered by expectations, relaxed, at ease. But I'm not. Already I hear my heart pounding in my ears like ominous music warning about the monster of a day looming over me. I'm filled with dread and can't make a decision about what I should do next. Without consciously deciding, I pick up my notebook and pen from my bedside table and draw one of Val's stupid triangles and think about what I'm thinking. I title my triangle *Starting the Day* and write:

Thoughts:

I don't know how to live today right.

Whatever I do/accomplish won't be enough (for who?)

I don't know how to be productive or efficient enough.

If I live my life/day wrong, not according to other people's expectations, I will disappoint them (who?).

I know, kind of, how I want my life/day/house/yard etcetera to go, and I am happy/content with that until I start to compare or think about how others (who?) will view/judge it.

I don't think there is enough time to get things done AND do what I want to do (what do I want to do?)

Feelings:

Apprehension, anxiety, indecision, loss of focus.

Behaviour:

Stalling.

Not living *my* life.

Not thinking about how I want to live my life.

After writing this down, I examine what I've written and add the following thoughts:

There is no right or wrong way to spend/live a day.

No one is evaluating/judging how I live my life.

If they are, there are no consequences. Noticing is enough.

At the bottom I add:

PERFECTION

ENOUGH

By which I mean perfection is the issue and feeling like I am enough is the solution.

I read through my triangle. I think about mornings. I think about ninth grade. I start to put it together. I think the reason I have morning dread may be because during that time my threat system was activated so regularly my body got the message that waking up equals inevitable threat. Maybe my struggle isn't about how to live my day productively, but rather how I am possibly going to get through the day so I don't encounter the threat. And maybe my brain seized on messages from my family and society about productivity and perfection, and I thought that if I was productive enough, perfect enough, then I could avoid the danger. I would be safe. Maybe my brain searched for a solution, and this is the one it chose. But the solution was impossible. Unattainable. There is no perfect life, and I think another part of me realized the futility: because there is no way to live perfectly, I can never do enough, let alone do enough perfectly to keep me safe. And if I can't keep myself safe, why get out of bed and even try?

I feel better after writing the triangle, less afraid, more empowered, as if shedding light on the day monster evaporated it. My heart rate normalizes. The ominous music stops. I get out of bed.

I start to do triangles often. Whenever I feel myself hung up, unable to move forward, stuck. These are some of the topics I cover: Going to the bookstore. Going to the grocery store. Making a phone call to a store to see if they have something in stock. Leaving the house. Clothes shopping. Going for a bike ride. Four p.m. and everyone is coming back home for the day. Housework. Not doing anything. Sale at a clothing store. Getting enough done today. Getting a call from a co-worker. Saying the wrong thing. Standing up for myself. Going to see Val. Sending an email to someone.

After a week of triangles, while sitting on my bed with a soft summer breeze wafting through the room, I review my journal and notice the common themes of perfectionism, and not being or having enough. When I look beneath the surface of those two themes another theme emerges: unworthiness. If I'm not perfect, then I'm not worthy. If I don't have enough—if I'm not enough—then I'm not worthy. And I immediately see how I place so much importance on external markers in my life in an attempt to make myself worthy. Things like having the right clothes. The right haircut. The right house. Being the right type of housekeeper. Being the right type of mother, wife, daughter and sister. Being the right type of employee. Thinking the right thoughts. Having the right ideas. And sometimes, I have moments of perfection in each of those areas, which bring moments of relief, but it is always temporary. There is no such thing as living perfectly, which I logically know, but can never accept because if there is no such thing as living perfectly, then how am I ever going to be able to be worthy enough? If I'm not worthy enough, then how can I ever keep myself safe? If I was worthy enough in ninth grade, it would never have happened to me. In ninth grade something must have been wrong with me for the boy to target me, and something must have been wrong with me for the teacher to not protect me.

Unworthiness.

I write the word in big letters with an exclamation point and circle it.

Unworthiness.

I look inside myself and finally face it: a starved, unloved little girl curled up in the fetal position, arms wrapped around her shivering, emaciated, naked body, trying to keep warm. Deep grooves mark the spaces between her ribs. Her jaundiced, sunken eyes, rimmed with eggplant-coloured shadows, stare vacantly from under greasy matted hair. The sight of her makes me cringe and look away.

Makes me cry.

All these years I've been trying to clothe the little girl with perfection, but because perfection doesn't exist, she stayed naked and cold. All these years I've tried to force-feed her a steady diet of *trying to be good enough* without realizing her little body can't absorb it. All these years I've been hiding her away, pretending she's not there, trying not to let anyone get close enough to see her. See me. Scared the sight of me, the real me, will make people cringe and look away.

It hurts too much to look at her. I'm caught off guard by the revelation, like I've been conned all over again. I've been trying to portray myself as a fairly confident woman for so long that I hid the truth from myself. But now that I realize it, now that I accept it, I do the first thing I can think of: an internet search for how to increase worthiness. I find *What is Self-Worth and How Do We Increase it?* on positivepsychology. com. The article contains information about self-worth, as well as activities, worksheets, meditations, recommended books, quotes, and YouTube videos.

It also gives three examples of healthy self-worth. Each example describes a person who perhaps isn't as smart or doesn't perform as well as those around them but still has a strong sense of value, self-worth and self-acceptance.

My response to all three examples is *Yeah, that's not me.* If I don't think I'll be good at something, I don't try. If I try something and find out I'm not good at it, I quit, because I don't deserve to do something if I'm not good at it. I don't deserve to do something just for the enjoyment of it. If I think I've upset someone, the friendship is over because I don't deserve a friend if I make a blunder. If I make a mistake at work, I beat myself up for the rest of the block and shrink away from my co-workers, who I believe loathe me for my ineptitude. I also hold others to these impossible standards, which makes it hard for me to build intimate friendships. If I'm not good enough for them and they aren't good enough for me, there's no middle ground for a meaningful relationship.

To challenge the tug of perfectionism, I come up with two mantras: *I'm supposed to be imperfect* and *I'm supposed to make mistakes.* I prefer those versions over *It's okay to be imperfect* and *It's okay to make mistakes.* I feel that having *okay* in the phrase is hedging expectations, like the expectation is still to try to be perfect and try not to make mistakes. Replacing *okay* with *supposed* reinforces my humanness. That to be human *is* to be imperfect and make mistakes. The *okay* in the phrase suggests to me that I am acceptable despite my imperfections and mistakes, whereas the *supposed* claims that I am worthy and acceptable because of my imperfections and mistakes. It's a subtle difference, but it's a difference that works for me.

I also start to remind myself that I am innately worthy, that my worth doesn't need to be earned. I try to believe it, but the words feel small and hollow when I say them, and bounce right off me. I try to do the exercises provided in the worksheets, but I struggle with sitting down with them, not wanting to confront the little neglected girl inside me.

Then I go to Wanuskewin.

Wanuskewin Heritage Park is a Canadian National Heritage site located just outside of Saskatoon. It's the site where nomadic tribes congregated to hunt and gather and find protection from the winter winds. It is home to Canada's longest-running archeological dig, with finds of human habitation over 6,000 years old. The park includes a visitor welcome centre and six kilometres of trails.

I like to visit the park once a year, and ask Jeff to join me for this venture during the Month of Karin. They often have a dance performance, so I want to be sure we get there in time to see it. We make the fifteen-minute drive on a warm sunny day, the buildings and traffic becoming sparser the further from the city we go. We turn off the highway onto a township road that leads us to the long approach cutting through the smooth prairie to the visitor centre. The low-profile building sided with wood blends into the landscape. We walk the main path to the front doors, passing a sculpture of three bronze buffalo in mid-charge. Once inside, we learn the performance is delayed, so we go for a walk on the trails. The groomed dirt paths take us past a grouping of teepees nestled among trembling aspen and Manitoba maple trees.

We amble along the creek cutting its way through the valley. A mother duck leads her paddling of chirruping ducklings into a stand of cattails. We cross paths with a few people. My heart rate increases as they get closer and spikes as we pass. We make our way up the valley and rest at a lookout to take in the mottled green beauty of the landscape.

When we return to the visitor centre, the dance performance is already under way. A small crowd sits around the circular stage. In the middle stands a Cree jingle dress dancer wearing a bright red dress with purple, yellow, blue and pink patterned accents. She has a thick black belt with silver studded geometric shapes. Lines of silver metal cones dangle closely together around the yoke of the bodice and the skirt. Her long dark hair is in two braids wrapped in red and purple ribbons. Her jewellery, headband, and moccasins are intricately beaded. She has a tall white feather fastened upright at the back of her head and carries a fan of black feathers with beaded quills. She's finishing a dance when Jeff and I arrive. We sit in the far back seats, in case I need a quick guilt-free getaway.

The dancer begins to talk about the history of jingle dress dancing. It is considered a healing dance. She talks about her own need for healing. She works with at-risk youth, who sometimes act out in violence towards her. She tells us that at first she thought it was part of her job to bear the physical brunt of their frustration. She knew it was because they had deeply troubled pasts. She didn't think it should have an effect on her, but she soon became so worn out by the trauma inflicted on her that she needed to take time off from work. She talks about believing that the world needs healing. Her hope and intention are that in some small way, her dancing can promote that healing. She talks about her fan of feathers. When she lifts them up to the sky, she is calling on the higher power to bring healing to whoever needs it. She explains that when she lifts up her other hand, she is inviting anyone who is watching to think of something they need, and her hand is up in honour of that intention, in agreement of that need, in support of it. She invites us to think of a word or something we may need, and to say it in our minds when she lifts up her hand.

Usually, my first instinct when hearing talk like this is instant dismissal. But instead of automatic skepticism, a word immediately comes to mind: *worthiness*. And I want it so desperately to stick to me, and she is so sincere, that all my doubts dissolve. When the drumming and singing begins, I sit on the edge of my chair waiting for her to raise her hand. She moves quickly around the stage with short up-and-down steps, turns back and forth and around.

She lifts up the feather fan and then, at a crescendo of drumming and singing, lifts up her other hand, and in my mind, I see the word *worthiness*. And then, with her hand in the air, and the word in my mind, worthiness doesn't just deflect or roll off, instead, it goes straight to my soul and envelops the little girl inside. Comforting her loneliness, cradling her sadness. I feel warmth and expansion in my chest as the little girl responds, drinks it in, absorbs her innate worth. I feel like I've found it, my worthiness, the beginning of it, the edges of it. Along with it comes the relief of finding it when I didn't believe I could ever have it, no matter how many times I repeated a mantra, tried to believe. My beginning to accept my worthiness begins to feed the little girl inside me and every time the dancer raises her hand, I don't just say the word in my mind, I start to believe it, and with the strengthening of that belief, my worthiness grows and the little girl recovers a little more.

After the performance, Jeff and I hang back while people from the audience approach the dancer to have a word.

When everyone clears out, I approach her, tears welling up in my eyes, my chest heavy with appreciation, and I let her know that what she said and what she did touched me. I point at my heart as I say it, then make a quick getaway to the bathroom to take a moment.

Over the next few weeks, when I notice the feeling of unworthiness, I picture the jingle dress dancer, hand high in the air in agreement to my worthiness, sending the word into my soul. And I feel it: an opening, a warmth, a release of the negative belief that I am unworthy, a growing acceptance that I am worthy.

And during these weeks, when I feel the pull of perfection, the sharp pain from the shame of making a mistake or remembering mistakes made, the guilt of past actions, of not being who I should have been, not being who I should be, I remember my mantras: *I'm supposed to be imperfect, I'm supposed to make mistakes.* I remind myself that I haven't been fooling anyone into believing that I am perfect. That my many mistakes are on public record, and in spite of that I have many people in my life who still love me, who are still kind to me, who still keep me safe, who still stay friends with me, who still treat me with respect, who, even if they don't like me, are still polite to me, and still tolerate me. And when I remind myself of all of that, I feel warmth and expansion in my chest as my worthiness replicates. My heart grows lighter as I shed the weight of my ideas of unattainable perfection. And I realize no one else is expecting me to be batting a thousand in this life, so I can let go of the expectation as well.

And as the weeks go on, I start to notice. I notice that if I make a mistake on a call at work, I don't beat myself up about it, and then withdraw into my shell, thinking that everyone now hates me, and no one wants to associate with a loser like me anymore. Instead, I notice that when I make a mistake, I accept it, do my best to correct it, and move on. I realize a mistake doesn't mean I'm a bad person, an unworthy person to be shunned; it's just a mistake.

I start to notice if I'm not my best self with my family or friends, or if I say something I regret, it doesn't haunt me like it used to. I don't wake up in the middle of the night in a cold sweat because I've done or said something so awful that I no longer deserve to have safety in the relationship. Instead, I notice that maybe I could have handled things differently. I'm able to have a conversation about it, let the other person be mad about it.

Let me be mad about it, if necessary, apologize if appropriate and move on. I no longer think I don't deserve their friendship anymore. I don't pull away, ignore phone calls and texts. I don't go into my cave of *safely alone*. Instead, I try to stay connected.

And I also notice that as I start to expect less of myself, I start to expect less of others. I get less irritated at mistakes, misdeeds, words misspoken. I'm more okay when I think someone is mad or disappointed in me. I make allowances. I'm more at ease.

And I start to notice that no one is noticing me when I'm walking down the street, getting groceries, checking out a book at the library, mailing a letter. They may see me, may interact with me, but I'm a blip on their screen, not a target in their sights. I find myself packing my bags at the grocery store and my heart isn't racing. My breath isn't shallow. My face and neck aren't red and splotchy. My armpits aren't soaked in sweat, and I think, *this must be what grocery shopping might feel like for other people.* And I'm amazed. I look around to see if anyone else is noticing how I'm packing my bags, just like them, like normal people.

I want to tell the cashier as she hands me my receipt, *Hey, this was a normal experience for me. I'm packing my bags and not freaking out inside.* And I want her to say, *Good job, kiddo!* But I have to be satisfied with my own satisfaction, as I roll my cart out of the store, head held high, Cheshire grin on my face, feeling extremely proud of myself.

After the Month of Karin, a month of triangles, mantras and visions of the jingle dress dancer, I see Val and she asks me how my anxiety levels are and a number comes to me that feels right.

"I'd say I'm 80% less anxious."

"Wow, that's something." Her face breaks into a wide smile.

That is something indeed.

13

It is a weekday at the end of September and I'm driving to my parents' home. They live in a small resort town seventy miles from the nearest airport. The traffic thins out the closer I get. Stands of green pine interspersed with maple, birch, and oak line the highway. Their broad green leaves are beginning to change into shades of a sunset sky. I take the exit leading to town. The woods bordering this road are dense and I keep an eye out for deer. I tune the radio to the local station, expecting to hear the same songs it played when I was in high school. It doesn't disappoint.

I pass by the old Mini-Putt: a sprawling mini-golf course with faded windmills and worn-out greens. Every hole has a challenge, an obstacle, a trick. Time your stroke just right to make it past the windmill blade. Take the easy shot on the wide ramp to guarantee making it onto the green, or risk the narrow ramp with the guaranteed hole in one. I drive by Putt Paradise, the new mini-golf course next door with its preformed mountain, waterfalls and shrubbery. All form, no substance.

I drive past the party store and fruit market on my left, resorts and the lake on my right. I open my window and breathe it in. It used to be, when I came to visit, as I drove into town something would settle in me: a feeling of relaxing on a molecular level, my atoms recognizing I'm home. But I've now lived longer in Saskatoon than I have here, and my body has a new home allegiance.

I turn at the first main intersection and pass my dad's old grocery store with its vacant windows staring out at the road. I pass the trailer park and turn onto the road leading to my parents' house. I drive slowly down two blocks filled with a mixture of permanent and vacation homes, nothing big, nothing fancy, all nestled in among pine and deciduous trees taller than anything in Saskatchewan.

My parents' house comes into view. It's a two-storey butter-coloured house nestled in among the trees. The front yard is meticulously landscaped with a long berm of blooming perennials, of which my mother will give me my annual tour, naming plants and flowers, pointing out what thrived, what died, what needs to be thinned by hand, what the deer thinned without permission. I park the rental car in the driveway and look to my left, through a small window with white lace curtains and a decorative bobble hanging from the curtain rod, to see if I can catch a glimpse of my mom at her piano. Instead, I hear the low hum of a hymn and I look further into the room to see her small upright frame working at the keys and pedals of the organ.

The porch door swings open and Dad comes out, wearing his usual blue jeans and a T-shirt with a pocket. His silver hair is still thick, his shoulders still broad and strong, his face open and wide with a smile. I love this, his *happy to see me* look. I get out of the car.

"Karin!"

"Dad!" He wraps me in his arms.

The organ music stops. Mom's face appears at the window. She waves and hustles away. Dad surveys my rental vehicle, asks how it handles. I go to grab my bag out of the trunk; he won't let me carry it.

"Is this all you have?"

"Yup."

He shakes his head in wonder that my mom never learned to travel so light. Astonished at the difference between us.

"Karin!" Smiling, Mom walks towards me, arms open wide.

"Mom!" I have to lean down to hug her tiny frame, careful not to hug too tight. She seems so fragile, but her strong hands grip my shoulders as she steps back to have a look at me, drinking me in and giving me her *what a lovely daughter I have* look.

"Look how long your hair's gotten." Mom reaches up and runs the ends of my hair through her fingers.

Mom leads me inside; Dad takes my bag upstairs, and then goes outside to start the grill for the massive steaks he bought from the meat market earlier today. There is potato salad and coleslaw and foil packets filled with grilled vegetables. We eat. We chit. we chat. We clean up. We watch a movie. Mom and I usually stay up late and talk on my first night. But tonight, I'm tired from travelling and I want to get a good night's sleep. I like to wake up early when I'm home.

I go to bed but I can't sleep. Things have been going well. I extended the Month of Karin indefinitely. I didn't go back to lawn bowling or clogging. I limit other plans and social interactions. I say *no* a lot more. I cut back on caffeine. Once my nervous system settled, once I could feel the calm of my baseline, once I wasn't racked with symptoms of anxiety hourly, once I learned to feel what it felt like to not be on alert all the time, I started to notice how my daily two cups of coffee triggered physical symptoms. It didn't just help me feel alert: it put me on guard. It made my heart pound, my pores sweat, my breathing shallow, all signals to my subconscious that something was wrong, because my body didn't yet know the difference between good energy and bad energy. It couldn't read the difference between excitement and threat. So, I decided to quit caffeine. Cold turkey.

Day one, I was a little tired, a little headachy, nothing a nap and ibuprofen couldn't fix. Day two, the headache morphed into a throbbing metronome of pain tapping the front and back of my head. I piggybacked acetaminophen with ibuprofen, but it didn't touch the discomfort. I persevered because the symptoms caffeine triggers are worse. On the third day, I woke up to find the metronome had transformed into a wrecking ball rhythmically thrashing my skull. I tried to divert my attention from the pain by lying on the couch watching television. By the afternoon, I started to feel nauseous, and eventually vomited three times. I gave up, had a cup of weak green tea and recovered immediately.

After my failed attempt, I decided to wean myself slowly, starting with three-quarters of a cup twice a day for a week, then half a cup, then a quarter, which I still have. Some mornings, the quarter cup triggers the symptoms of anxiety. Some mornings, I just feel a little more alert and energized with no symptoms. My body is learning.

But even when my anxiety flares up, things are better. I recognize it sooner. I intervene more quickly. I wind down faster. And the times in between the flare-ups are longer, neutral, with small windows of enjoyment. Times when I feel like the person I was meant to be, the person who I suspected I was, but couldn't bring forward, because I was trapped in a pattern of constant reactions to imaginary threats. I told all of this to Val in our meeting earlier this month and she asked me if I'd thought about how I would know when it's time to stop seeing her.

"Yeah, I've thought about it and I feel like this should be the last one."

Val nodded and smiled as if she suspected the same thing.

"I just feel like I've got a pretty good handle on things, that I understand what is going on well enough, and that now it's just going to take some time for things to get better, more so than talking about it. I feel like I understand how what happened to me affected me, and that it's not my fault."

"I'm glad you said that." Val sat up alertly. "It's important for you to know that it wasn't your fault."

"Oh yeah," I said. More like, oh duh. "I've never thought it was my fault."

Val smiled. We talked a bit about what comes next: how I can always come back if I need to. She explained that healing isn't a straight line, but an up-and-down journey. She told me she thinks I'm an interesting person and extended her hand to shake hands with Karin, the real Karin, no longer hidden by overwhelming anxiety.

Part of me didn't want our meetings to end. But while I'm a little scared of venturing out on my own, I'm also wary of turning Val into a crutch. Val walked me out of her office and we stood in the waiting room for an awkward moment listening to the bubbling aquarium and soft rock music.

"It feels like we should hug." I screwed up my face as if it were a question and not a statement.

Val closed her eyes briefly and nodded solemnly.

"I think we should hug." Arms open, she stepped towards me and wrapped me in a hug as warm and soft as her smile and we said goodbye.

So, here I am, flying solo, Val-free, visiting my parents. I'd like to say that leading up to the trip I felt excited or even neutral, but I'm not that far along in my *healing journey* yet, as evidenced by the nine hundred dollars' worth of clothing I spent too much time looking for, and buying in anticipation of doing something outside the confines of my tepid life. I can't yet tolerate the feeling that only shopping can take away.

And the lead-up to this visit brought up questions. Questions like, should I report what happened to me to the police? I waffle back and forth on it. My reason for reporting it isn't to have it investigated, just to have it on record; because, what if he did it to other people? What if his behaviour escalated into something else? Something worse? Do I have a responsibility to report if it points to a pattern? Some days I am convinced it is the right thing to do. Other days, I picture myself walking into the police station, and the locusts in my stomach flare up, convincing me it's not a good idea.

And then there is the question of whether I tell Mom and Dad. My oldest brother? My sister? Part of me longs to tell them what happened. How it affected me. How hard it's been. Most days I'm resolved that I'll never tell them. Why spread the pain? Other days I think I might, and when I picture myself telling them, my heart begins to pound out its objection. I'm not sure why.

Tonight, in the upstairs bedroom of my parents' house, the desire to tell them pulls me away from sleep. Possible monologues of what I would say swirl around in my brain until I finally sit up, turn on the light, pull out my journal and scribble all the things I want to tell, share with them. I scribble until my fingers cramp and all my thoughts are exorcised out of my head and onto the page. I close my journal, and toss it on the floor, turn out the light, and lay my head on the pillow. But still the words: *tell, don't tell, tell, don't tell, tell, don't tell* swing back and forth through my brain until I fall asleep.

The next morning, I wake up. I'm in my brother's old bedroom. The bedroom that used to have bunk beds and gerbils. The bedroom from which the sounds of Steve practising his drums and Dave strumming "Smoke on the Water" used to emanate. The bedroom to which I carried my pillow and dragged my blanket in order to sleep beside their beds, because falling asleep alone in my room was too scary.

A card table stands next to the bed, with the current puzzle Dad and Mom are working on. It's the one I sent to him for Father's Day, pictures of different types of chickens with quotes such as, *Roosters don't give a cluck*. I look forward to working on the puzzle with them later, and hearing Dad say things like, "Look at this funny piece," and "This piece goes somewhere."

There is a wooden bookshelf beside the puzzle table with sixty years' worth of photo albums lining the shelves, along with other books, framed photos, knickknacks from travels. My favourite is an orange wooden folk-art horse painted with flowers. I'm always tempted to pack it in my bag when I leave, but I never do. There is a large closet with sliding wooden doors, usually packed with clothes and boxes. Mom has carved out a space for me to hang my things on the left-hand side. The right-hand side is where the gun used to be. I never open that side of the closet even though I know it's not there anymore.

I check the time, 6:12 a.m. I'm not too late. I roll out of bed and walk into the hall where Dad's desk sits against a wall. Above the desk is a photo of his police college graduating class. I pick him out of all the other men with crew cuts. He's so young. On his desk is a Rolodex of photos. The photo on display in front is of my nephews, Steve's boys. I flip through the photos and replace my nephews with Maddie and Max. I walk past my old bedroom, which has been turned into Mom's gym. I go down the stairs lined with family photos. Dave's, Steve's, my sister's and my school portraits are hung in order. I stop and look at mine. I reach out and touch ninth-grade Karin's smiling face. She was so young.

I head to the kitchen. Mom has marked my place at the kitchen table with a cloth napkin rolled up in a silver napkin ring, engraved with my name. Next to the napkin is a framed photo of Mom and Dad. Leaning against the frame is a white envelope with my name in Mom's handwriting. I open it. It is their last will and testament. Weird. I notice, on the lazy Susan, a clear container filled with white powder. On the top of the container is a note in Mom's handwriting: "This is not sugar." Weirder. I take a picture of it and send it to my co-workers, with the caption, "What do you think it is?"

I hear the TV on in the family room, so I know I'm not too late. I microwave a mug of water and take it to Dad's instant coffee station on the corner of the counter. I dole out some dark crystals of coffee and light crystals of sugar, give it a stir and go to the living room, where Dad is sitting at the end of the couch.

"Hey! Karin!" Dad, smiling big, puts down his paper.

"Hey, Dad."

I sit in the adjacent armchair. Dad picks up his paper, switching his attention between it and the TV. And here, sitting near Dad, sipping our instant coffees, watching TV, is one of my favourite parts of my trip home: for these few days, in moments like this, I get my dad all to myself.

On the TV is Dad's favourite morning show, featuring a pretty blonde woman in a short colourful dress, flanked by two older men in suits and ties. They sit on a white sofa. A seasonal bouquet of flowers rests on the coffee table in front of them. The show is *Fox and Friends*. It's the only time I watch the program.

Dad and I differ in our political views. While he leans right, I lean left. Watching *Fox and Friends* is a springboard into friendly political debates. He knows how to needle and push my buttons with a smile. It's frustrating fun at its best. We both end up sticking to our positions, without necessarily believing or agreeing with all we are saying. Our debates aren't about coming to consensus, they're about having the better argument, about winning. I'm not sure which of the positions Dad takes in these arguments that he actually believes. Belief is beside the point. But sometimes I wish we could take a step back from our sides, our arguments, and talk about what we think is really important: what we really believe.

I wish we could have done that during my visit three years ago while Dad sat on the couch, and I sat in the armchair. We sipped our instant coffee and watched a breaking story on *Fox and Friends*. That was the first week of October 2016. Trump was the Republican presidential candidate, and Dad and I had already had a few lively debates about him.

That morning, news had broken about a released recording of Donald Trump. The recording took place in 2005 between Access Hollywood anchor Billy Bush and Donald Trump. On the recording, Donald Trump's unmistakable voice is heard saying, "I better use some Tic Tacs just in case I start kissing her. You know I'm automatically attracted to beautiful—I just start kissing them. It's like a magnet. Just kiss. I don't even wait. And when you're a star they let you do it. You can do anything. Grab them by the pussy. You can do anything."

Hearing those words, I was immediately transported to ninth-grade metal shop class, and felt the boy seize me. Restrain me. Grab me by the pussy. I remembered how he did it whenever he wanted. How he believed he could just do anything. It was one of the few times I'd recalled it.

The first time I'd thought about it was a few summers after graduation. I was home on break from college and had gone to meet up with a friend at a local bar. I was standing at the counter waiting for a drink when the boy, now technically a man, sidled up to me. Same feathered brown hair, same smile.

He wanted to talk about old times, reminisce. "Do you remember giving me this?" He pointed to a scar on his hand.

I remembered. We were in shop class and I was using a scriber, which is a sharp metal tool, to etch a pattern on a piece of sheet metal for the toolbox I was making. My left hand was holding the sheet metal in place while my right hand used the scriber to score lines in it when the boy crept up next to me with his your-hands-are-busy-let's-play grin on his face. Without thinking, I reached over and slashed him with the scriber, carving a deep groove into the palm of his hand. He pulled his hand away and jumped back, a look of surprise plastered on his face.

I felt no vindication, no victory, no satisfaction. I hadn't been plotting how to keep myself safe, or planning my revenge. I didn't feel hate for the boy. Our daily encounters had become so regular, so normal, so nothing, that I didn't even think about them. But I guess a part of me had had enough.

My eyes followed the boy as he walked straight towards the teacher, showed him the gaping wound and then pointed at me. I remember the teacher looking at the gash, then looking at me.

I remember staring back, eyes dull, expression flat, not attempting to defend my actions. I don't remember if the teacher said anything to the boy. But I remember what the teacher did to me. Nothing.

And that nothingness—no action, no correction, no warning to me—when I had wilfully misused a dangerously sharp tool to cut a fellow classmate, was how I knew the teacher understood that what the boy did to me, under his watch, was wrong.

The boy, now a man, stood next to me in the bar, finger pointing to the scar. As what? A badge of the good times we'd had together in shop class? Did he show this scar off to other people? Did he tell a story about it? Did the story it come with a smile? Was I the villain in it? I didn't know what he was looking for. An apology? Contrition? A shared laugh at my foolish impulsiveness? It seemed like he wanted something from me.

"You deserved it." I locked eyes with him before walking away.

I didn't think of him again until decades later.

After first telling Val about my *life event*, I wondered why the realization of its significance had to happen so suddenly. Why it had to be such a shock. Why my brain couldn't have eased me towards it. Gently edging my way into it like walking into a cold lake. Why I wasn't better prepared when I got pushed off my nice dry dock of denial.

Now, almost a year after spilling my life event out to Val, sitting with Dad watching *Fox and Friends,* I realize that my brain was trying to tell me something, it was trying to get me ready, prepare me. I was just too dense to notice what was going on.

Three years ago, sitting in the armchair next to Dad, listening to the recording of Donald Trump bragging about how he just grabs women by the pussy, part of me was transported back to shop class, trapped between the boy's biceps, his hands all over me, all my classmates' eyes on me, feeling overwhelmed with waves of shame, frozen in place, heart racing, holding my breath—and another part of me was watching Dad. Trying to gauge his reaction. Looking for a shake of the head, a scowl, a grunt of disgust in judgement of the words spoken by the Republican candidate for the President of the United States.

Dad turned to the next page of the newspaper as if the breaking news meant nothing.

I sat there, still paralyzed by my flashback. Stunned that Donald Trump's words seemed meaningless to my dad. And I needed to know. I needed to know what he really thought about what Donald Trump bragged about.

"What if that happened to Mom?" Blood rushed to my face and neck, mottling them with red splotches. "What if some guy suddenly came up to her and started grabbing her, started kissing her?"

Dad just stared at me. Probably because he didn't want to lose a point in our ongoing debate about the upcoming election. Probably because he didn't think my seventy-eight-year-old mother was in danger of anyone kissing and groping her.

But right then I didn't care about winning or losing, I didn't care about our debate, the only thing I wanted to hear was that those words aren't just locker room talk, they are reprehensible. That no self-respecting man would do that to a woman, much less be pathetic enough to think that bragging about it would earn him approval. That it is not okay to just grab someone by the pussy. That my dad would beat the shit out of anyone who grabbed my mom like that. Because maybe, if he would beat up someone who did that to Mom, then maybe he would have stopped the boy. I sat there, waiting for my dad to say those things. But he didn't say anything.

I couldn't sit there any longer. I stormed out of the room, went into the bathroom, slammed the door and burst into tears.

Shortly after that visit, I saw Val for the very first time. But I hadn't put it all together. And I hadn't even thought to tell her about the boy and ninth grade. I thought the unhinged feeling I had, the increased anxiety, had to do with my job, and after three sessions of her being very kind and affirming, and some distance between me and the U.S. election, and the world not spontaneously combusting at the craziness of it all, I felt I didn't need to see her anymore.

But the events of ninth grade started popping into my head more frequently. I began to tell it to my friends and co-workers. Then they began to tell me their stories too. But that is all they seemed to be, just stories of brief injustice, not trauma, not lasting effects.

And then came Kavanaugh.

Before Trump, I had never paid much attention to politics, and before Kavanaugh, I never paid any attention to the Supreme Court nominations. But when Brett Kavanaugh was nominated to the Supreme Court, and Christine Blasey Ford came forward alleging that he had sexually assaulted her when they were teenagers, I became obsessed with following every news story regarding it.

It lasted for weeks. I kept telling myself to stop watching, take a break from the news, there's nothing you can do about it, nothing you can change. But I was compelled. I wanted to see how the senators would vote. It was during this time that I started feeling unwell. I had sore throats that threatened to build into a cold. I had constant chest heaviness, and pain. I felt dull and fatigued. I had a hard time concentrating, and was not on my usual game at work. Most days of work I debated calling in sick. I stopped exercising and cancelled plans I'd made with friends. At first, I thought it was just the precursor of an illness, the flu or a cold, but when other symptoms never appeared, I thought maybe it was stress. Maybe ten years of answering 911 had caught up with me. Maybe I needed to go see Val. So, I made an appointment.

Then it came time for Christine Blasey Ford to testify. I watched intently, found myself nodding, understanding her on a wordless, instinctual level. Still, I wasn't surprised when Kavanaugh passed the nomination.

My main feeling when it was over was relief. Now I could stop watching the news. I did, and I started to feel better, so much so that I considered cancelling my appointment with Val. But I didn't, and ever since then a question has dug its way into me: Why didn't I tell my dad what happened?

Sometimes the question was, *Why didn't I tell my parents?* but it was never just, *Why didn't I tell my mom?* I'm not sure why. Maybe because I didn't think that as a woman in 1980s, she would have had any power. Maybe because I thought if I told her, she would have told Dad and together they would have made a decision about what to think or do. I just don't know.

When I asked Val the question, *Why didn't I tell anyone?* she replied that I had already told the most powerful person I knew: the teacher. And because telling him hadn't helped, it would be natural for me to not consider telling anyone else.

Her answer made sense, but it didn't free me from the question. The answer felt much more slippery and deep than that. Like I was trying to grab on to a bar of soap from a large tub of swirling murky water, but my hand could only touch the edge of the bar before it shot away.

But now, three years after watching the breaking news about Trump and the Access Hollywood tapes on *Fox and Friends* with Dad, and one year after revealing my *life event* to Val, I'm here again, sitting next to Dad, sipping on a mug of instant coffee, pretending to be interested in his morning show.

The water suddenly clears, and the answer rises to the top. I didn't tell him because I didn't *want* to know what he would say, what he would do.

If the teacher, *a very moral man*, who is a respected church-going member of the community, whose nice and well-behaved sons worked with me, who witnessed the boy harass me, didn't help me, then maybe my dad wouldn't have helped me either. If the teacher, most of my classmates, and the boy didn't think anything was wrong with what was happening, then maybe my dad wouldn't think anything was wrong either. If the teacher didn't punish me for cutting the boy because he thought the boy deserved it, then maybe the reason he didn't punish the boy for assaulting me was because he thought I deserved it. And if the teacher thought I deserved it, then maybe my dad would have too.

If I told my dad, and he dismissed it as *boys will be boys*, if he didn't think it was a problem, if he thought it was normal, or a joke, if he didn't think I was worth protecting, I think that would have crushed me, broken me completely, and some part of my brain couldn't take that chance; thought it was just better not to know.

I look over at Dad, his nose deep into the newspaper, rightly oblivious to my internal struggle. It's not fair to him. It's not his fault. He didn't know. He never had the chance to respond.

I want to tell him what happened. Ask him what he would have done. But he's eighty-one years old, and while my wounds are finally starting to heal, I'm afraid of hurting him with my story. And even if I could be assured that by telling him I wouldn't hurt him, the part of me with a deep groove of doubt worn into my belief system by the teacher's indifference stiffens at the thought, is skeptical of the chances of hearing the answer I need to hear, and pushes the question down through my brain, through my throat, spine and tailbone, into the chair, through the floor and the foundation deep into the ground where it can be consumed by worms, and excreted into the soil.

I sit there, watching my dad, privileged to be a welcome part of his morning ritual, and I feel my heart burn with hatred for the teacher who taught me to doubt my dad.

14

Back in Saskatoon it's mid-October and Mother Nature has treated the city to an early gift of snow, which covers the carpet of leaves Jeff and I kept saying we'd take care of "next week." We tell ourselves it will be good for the grass to get a little leaf decay, a little compost. It's a clean slate. That is kind of what my life feels like now and I'm trying to figure out what activities I actually like. Figuring out how I want to spend my time, where to put my energies that are now mostly free due to the extension of the Month of Karin, which has turned into the Four Months of Karin without any anxiety-inducing extra-curricular activities. Small outings like the library, groceries, the pharmacy are more predictable, fairly symptom-free.

I feel like I am in neutral, a really nice, easy boring neutral. It's becoming so boring and so easy that sometimes I think I am ready to do more. My co-workers and I talk about playing pickleball. We used to play it regularly last year but it fell to the wayside. We schedule three gym times. I can't bring myself to go to any. In moments of inner space and ease, I think how nice it would be to invite a couple over to play cards or board games, but I can't bring myself to even suggest it to Jeff.

I do start one pastime: writing. I sit down with my notebook or at my computer, and I become absorbed in the process of documenting, creating, and reorganizing my thoughts. I begin writing short fiction and creative non-fiction. I start to think I could use some help, some guidance, a writing community. I go online in search of one, and join the Saskatchewan Writers'

Guild. I apply to participate in their three-day, facilitated writers' retreat and am excited when I receive my notice of acceptance. I look forward to it for weeks. I don't go clothes shopping in preparation. I pack what I have. I feel like I'm not just acting like a normal person, I think I'm feeling like one. Until I start driving.

It's a ninety-minute drive to St. Peter's Abbey, where the retreat is held. The empty highway cuts through the snow-covered fields glistening under the bright blue sky, and all my familiar symptomatic friends begin to rear their ugly heads. My heart thumps against the tension of the seat belt, sweat seeps through the armpits and crotch of my clothing. My neck twitches and contorts. I try to calm myself. I say my mantras. I do a mental triangle. They are little help against my strong-willed friends.

Still, I persist. I endure. I park. I unpack. I meet the facilitator and other participants at dinner. I act normal. I make it through. I go my room where, crying and shaking, I pace the floor for most of the night debating: do I stay, do I go, do I stay, do I go. I want to stay because I want to be a person who can do something she wants to do, but my body doesn't much care what I want. Instead, my heart churns my nerves and blood into a tornado that keeps touching down all over my body, making me sweat and jump at every sound. And yet I can't bring myself to leave in the middle of the night. I can't bear to publicly fail, so I barely sleep for two nights, white-knuckle the group sessions and learn my lesson that just because I want to do something, just because I think I should be able to do it, doesn't mean I can. And after the retreat, I give up trying, shift back into neutral and hope it's enough.

Jeff isn't a tough sell on lying low in life. His general level of contentment is so high it suspiciously resembles apathy. Still, I check in with him every now and then.

"Have I become too boring?" I corner him one day in the kitchen.

He gives me a mischievous look. "Compared to what?"

"I don't know. Do you think we should go out more? Be more social? Have friends?" My eyes scan his face searching for clues to what he really thinks.

"There's no one I like more than you, so what does it matter?" He waves away my concern with a hand.

"You know what I mean."

"Listen." Jeff's voice assumes a tone of sincerity. "This is just one end of the pendulum. And it's okay for now. It won't last forever."

"No?" My voice rises in doubt.

"Probably not." The mischievous look returns to Jeff's face, signalling he would be content either way.

It's now been months since I've seen Val. Months since I've done a triangle, months since I've tried anything. After my last visit with her, I was tired of thinking about healing, moving forward, making progress. I was tired of noticing how much of my response to life is filtered through coping to deal with the trauma of *being sexually abused*. So, I put it in a box, placed it on a shelf, and kept my life to a mind-numbingly slow pace so I wouldn't have to think about it. The days grew shorter, darker and colder, and my life stayed small and easy, but when 2019 cleared away and the longer sunnier days of 2020 appeared, my energy rallied and I was ready for more. And more appeared in the form of an email inviting me to participate in the Public Safety Personnel Wellbeing Course, or PSP course for short.

The PSP course is free of charge, pairs participants with a therapist, and makes use of internet-based cognitive behavioural therapy (ICBT). Val's dreaded triangle that I first scoffed at but then later had success with is one component of ICBT. A structured program incorporating it sounded like a good way to get back into a routine of focusing on my mental health. There are five lessons in the course, which take at least eight weeks to complete. I wasn't sure if I'd be accepted as a participant because the issues I deal with didn't stem from work-related trauma.

Now, to be fair, my job doesn't help me either. Answering 911 and the police line for the last eleven years has had a significant impact on my core beliefs. If I was a nervous driving companion before I started, I am completely neurotic now because I hear about the accidents, the road rage, the distracted driving, the intoxicated people driving into oncoming traffic. If I was conscious of locking my vehicle and house before, I am militant about it now, locking my car doors after I've loaded up groceries to return the shopping cart to its rightful place ten feet away. I wake up in the morning and am always pleasantly surprised my car hasn't been vandalized, or my shed broken into. When I leave work after a particularly stabby night, I expect to see pools of blood on the sidewalks, and bodies in alleys on my drive home. I imagine it will be only a matter of time before I am bear-sprayed. My family is a little annoyed by my vigilance.

Jeff once talked about putting a driveway in front of our house. I was skeptical because there isn't much space.

"Cars run into buildings all the time." I pursed my lips and raised my eyebrows.

"All the time?" His eyebrows challenged me back.

"More than you'd think."

Not long after that, we went to pick up an order at a wine kit store in a nearby strip mall. The front window of the store was boarded up.

"I wonder how that happened." Jeff stood, hands on hips, surveying the damage.

"I bet a car ran into it." My eyebrows assumed their all-knowing position.

"I don't think so." Jeff pointed at the concrete parking block. I shrugged my shoulders. Once inside, we asked the clerk what had happened.

"Car ran into the building," he said with a wry smile.

"Really!" Jeff said.

"Third time it's happened." The clerk shook his head.

"Happens all the time." I crossed my arms and gave Jeff my best *why don't you ever believe me* look.

Since I've started noticing the toll trauma has taken, I've wondered if it's wise for me to continue working at the police station. I've wondered if it's possible to heal from three decades of unresolved trauma, and still be able to work in a job where I am exposed to secondary trauma hourly and not completely break. I feel where I'm weak. I have my doubts. But at the same time, my family is counting on my paycheque, my benefits. My pension will keep Jeff and me comfortable when I retire. And I don't think, with my limited skill set, I can find another job equal to this one. I'm hoping I'll be accepted into the PSP course, not just to kick me out of neutral, but to give me the tools I need to stay mentally healthy enough to keep my job.

I enroll in the course, answer questions on their online questionnaire and make an appointment for the phone screening. I'm accepted. I'm assigned a therapist, Janine. We communicate by email, but I have the option of talking with her on the phone by appointment as well. I'm nervous about beginning the course. The information on the PSPNET webpage says that *The Wellbeing course has shown success as a treatment for anxiety, depression, and post-traumatic stress disorder.* I'm worried that if it's not successful for me, I'm as healed as I can get.

Each lesson begins with a questionnaire to gauge my level of anxiety, depression, and PTSD. I tick off answers as accurately as I can, while at the same time thinking about what my answers would have been a year ago. The difference makes me realize how far I've already come, how much less broken I am. Janine sends me the results of my lesson one questionnaire: *Your symptoms of depression and anxiety are within the mild range....your scores are also clinically significant for symptoms of PTSD.* It sounds about right. I wonder what it would have been a year ago. I wonder what it would be like if I hadn't extended the Month of Karin.

The lessons are clear, informative, easy to follow, and include weekly tasks and instructions for simple skills. Deceptively simple skills. Skills that start to work almost immediately. After my week-two assessment, Janine writes that my *depressive and PTSD symptoms have reduced to within the healthy range.* My anxiety has remained the same, but she says it is not uncommon. In addition to the weekly lessons is a resource section covering topics such as Managing Beliefs, Assertive Communication, Panic Attacks and Strong Physical Sensations. I read the Anger resource last because I don't think it applies to me. I'm surprised to learn it applies more to me than I thought.

As I go through the course, I notice changes. I feel less reserved and guarded and more open and interactive in social encounters with my co-workers, store clerks, the librarian. Instead of being stuck in neutral, I begin to experience moments of real enjoyment instead of just feeling like I should be enjoying myself. I go to dinner and a movie with my friends, and am able to be in the moment, get lost in the movie, forget that there are other people in the restaurant, in the theatre. I feel less burnt out at work and accept an overtime shift for the first time in five years. I play pickleball with Jeff at the gym, and when four men start playing in the court directly behind me, and my old symptomatic friends begin to creep up on me, I use the skills from the course and stop them in their tracks.

The course is so helpful, so effective, I start preaching it to everyone I know at work. There is a similar Wellness Course for spouses or significant others that I regularly remind Jeff about. The information and skills in the course seem so instrumental for general well-being that I'm baffled it isn't recommended for every human being, just like eating healthy and exercising are recommended for physical health. But as Jeff often reminds me, there are none so righteous as the newly converted. So, I try to not pester him too much about it.

I'm feeling so much more optimistic, I look forward to putting what I've learned to the test. I have three events coming up in the next month: a full day of training, which involves being in the same room with approximately sixty people for twelve hours, Maddie's university graduation banquet, and a five-day trip to Calgary to help Maddie find an apartment. I make a plan to mitigate my symptoms, make a goal not to buy any new clothes, and use my new skills to stop myself from going down the rabbit hole of mindless online searching and shopping. I feel like it's finally going to happen. I'm finally going to be able to shift out of neutral. Venture outside my bubble and meet life with a little more balance, a little more ease. And then the World Health Organization declares the COVID-19 pandemic on March 11th. Saskatchewan goes into lockdown a week later, and all my best-laid plans are cancelled.

I'm not going to pretend that the lockdown is hard for me, that it's a struggle for me to stay at home and not go anywhere. Now that everyone in my city, my province, my country is forced into isolation, I feel a little more in step with the world, a lot less like I might be missing out on something. I've been training for life in the lockdown for the last year, and I settle right in. I order six puzzles and send Dad and Mom pictures of the ones I complete. Dad sends me a puzzle that he is working on, and we have a friendly competition to see who can complete it in the shortest time.

But while staying home isn't hard, the uncertainty of what is to come gnaws at me. My neck twitches and ribbits increase and pretty soon my closet fills up with grey Eddie Bauer shipping bags stuffed with online clothing purchases that don't fit. Hangers hold all the new purchases that do fit because it's important to dress correctly for the pandemic. Apparently.

I'm ashamed of the grey bags in my closet, disgusted with myself. I don't know why I can't kick this coping habit to the curb. Jeff tells me not to be so hard on myself, because it's not putting us in the poorhouse. I appreciate his understanding every time the boxy white FedEx truck appears, and the blue-and-purple-clad deliverer slips the package between the doors, which I sheepishly retrieve and scuttle away to my hidey hole. I appreciate that Jeff doesn't judge me, and in fact gives me permission to buy whatever I want, even if I don't need it or will never wear it, knowing that on the spectrum of coping, shopping is less harmful than other addictions. I'm aware of this too. But it still doesn't change the fact that I'm so sick of it, sick of its hold on me, sick of trying to challenge my thoughts, modify my behaviours, and not getting any closer to cracking the code of why I feel compelled to shop, shop, shop.

Clothes shopping is a regular feature of my thought-examining, one of the skills used in the PSP course. It's similar to Val's triangle.

But something else is competing for space in my thought-challenging journal these days: work drama. It is making my anxiety skyrocket. My mind spins with imaginary scenarios, conversations and arguments, so much so I haven't been able to sleep for the last two nights before my day shifts, and I am taking the night shifts off, not only because I'm exhausted, but because I'm recognizing I need a little space, a little perspective.

Now, I'm not going to get into the details of the actual work drama except to say it is a completely normal, unexceptional situation. One that has most likely played out in some form or another in every other workplace where there is an issue to be decided upon and there are two opposing arguments. The point isn't so much *what* the argument is as, it is *how much* it is affecting me. How invested I am in people agreeing with me, that my viewpoint is heard, understood, validated. How it doesn't seem like just a matter of opinion, but feels like a matter of life and death.

This isn't the first time I've felt this strongly about my way of seeing things. It's a lifelong pattern. It's not about my idea vs. their idea. It's me vs. them, and if they can't see my way of thinking, particularly if it's backed by science, logic, established rules, laws, policies and procedures, then I'm suspicious of them. I don't trust them. I feel betrayed by them, and I don't want them in my circle. It's probably the reason my circle is very small. But this time around, I'm starting to realize the problem isn't them, it's me.

I start to journal about it. About why I find certain arguments so personal, like an attack, like it affects my sense of personal safety. I start to think about ninth grade. I think about how I knew I didn't like what was happening. How I didn't want it to happen. How I thought it was wrong, and yet no one else seemed to know. Not the boy who seemed oblivious to my distress when I fought and yelled. Not the classmates, who stood by and watched me struggle. Not the teacher, who saw it happen and did nothing even when I asked him for help.

I start to think about how crazy-making it must have been for me to *know* what was happening was wrong, but not be able to convince anyone else it was wrong. But I *knew* I was right, so maybe the problem was that I couldn't convince them that what the boy was doing to me was wrong. And because I couldn't convince them, control them, manipulate them into seeing clearly what was happening, then maybe it was my fault.

It was my fault. Almost from day one I've told myself what happened wasn't my fault. Of course it wasn't my fault. I was a kid. I didn't ask for it. I didn't want it. How could it be my fault? That's what I thought because I know that is the right way to think about it. But now I realize, that is not what I believe.

It *was* my fault.

The thought swirls around the inside of my head like the penny in the donation funnel. My mind spins and I grow dizzy the closer it gets to the hole.

It was my fault.

The thought picks up speed, frantically circling the vortex until it finally drops into the black hole, taking me with it. My stomach drops as I fall into the knowledge that all this time I believed it was my fault.

Of course it was my fault. It was my fault because I should have known better than to take a shop class full of boys. It was my fault because I wore the wrong clothes, my hair was wrong, my makeup was wrong, I stood in the wrong spot, said the wrong thing, wasn't nice enough, wasn't smart enough, wasn't funny enough, wasn't careful enough, wasn't liked enough, wasn't good enough. Whatever it was, it was something I did or didn't do, and for the last three decades I've been trying to fix, or control, or do, or not do whatever it was that made the boy repeatedly sexually assault me.

It was my fault.

I see that belief as a black hole in the centre of my chest that drives so much of how I respond to the world around me, and pulls me ever inward, away from connection, love, and joy. I understand the importance of unearthing this belief. I don't try to tell myself I don't believe it or pretend it's not there. I recognize it. I accept it. I sit and stew in the knowledge of it. I see it as a part of me, as real and palpable as my kidney or stomach. I stare into it. Turn it around. Study it. I worry that the belief is too strong, too established to be conquered, but still, I make a plan.

I challenge. I journal. I breathe. I make new mantras, and the belief begins to starve and shrink as I feed myself new truths and plant new beliefs, which crowd it out. For all of its hold on me, the belief that it was my fault retreats surprisingly quickly, as if it can only flourish in the dark. I try to remember to keep the light on it.

I look back through my journaling about the work drama, and all of a sudden it doesn't matter; it really doesn't matter.

Whatever the outcome is, whatever decision is made, even if I don't like it, I know they aren't them, now isn't then. I can't control other people with what I do, what I say, what I wear, how I look, and I don't need to.

Because it wasn't my fault.

15

I t's June 21, 2020, Father's Day, and I'm dreaming. In one dream I am at a dinner party, at which, after a complicated pandemic hand-washing routine, I demonstrate to the host how to use his Instant Pot. I then find myself holding a plate of food in the middle of the kitchen, wondering where to sit because I don't know anyone. I see a seat available at a table. I tell myself I shouldn't sit there because I think the people there don't want to know me, won't like me. I then think, maybe they do, maybe they will, and I sit down. Then the dream transitions, and I am sitting in a movie theatre. A strange man puts his arm around my shoulders. I move his arm off of me and give him a disapproving glare. He tells me, "If you don't want my arm around you, then you should leave." I tell him, "No, you're the one that needs to go," and he does.

I wake up. Plod to the kitchen. Give Rosie a scratch, dish out her much-cried-for wet food, and make a cup of mostly decaf instant coffee. I have a little visit with Jeff and Maddie. I go for a short run because I've been finding the cardio helps release nervous energy. As my feet rhythmically slap the asphalt, I think about my dreams, how different they are now than a year and a half ago. How, like then, they are still trying to inform me. How now, I'm more apt to get the message. I think about my meeting with Val almost eighteen months ago, and how deep and thick the shadow of almost a lifetime of unresolved trauma seemed. How interwoven it was into every aspect of my life. How I wasn't sure I would have enough light to dispel the darkness. That even if I could untangle the ropes,

I wasn't sure there would be anything left of me: if it would be worth trying.

Thick herds of elephantine clouds migrate slowly eastward through the vast field of blue overhead. A bushy globe cedar vibrates with a large contingent of gossiping sparrows, and a tree, its arms spread wide, shows off its bursting pink blossoms. And I feel it: the vastness of the sky, the liveliness of the birds, the beauty of the tree. It's not a head knowledge, an *I should be appreciating this nice day* thought. It's an automatic response to pleasure, to feeling the earth's caress. It's my body, after years of trying to stay safe by blocking everything out, learning to trust, to let some things in.

I get home, make myself a smoothie, and drink it while I stretch my hamstrings, hips, calves and quads. I call Dad. Mom answers. Dad is at Tractor Supply getting chipmunk traps, but should be home in about fifteen minutes. Mom and I chat about her upcoming foot surgery. She had a broken toe a while back in which the doctor put in a screw. But the screw has worked its way out of the bone and is pushing against her skin. The doctor is going to remove the screw and inject something into the hole it left behind.

"What are they going to inject into it?" I move the phone to my other ear.

"I don't know."

"Foam insulation?" I'm smiling.

"Maybe." Mom's chuckling makes my smile grow.

I suggest that since Dad is pretty handy with screws and foam insulation, she might as well have him do it, and save herself a trip to the doctor. She says she'll take it under consideration. I catch her up on work, Jeff, the kids. I tell her I've been writing a book.

"Good," she says. "You've always been a good writer."

She tells me about a few pages of writing of mine that she reread recently. It was forty things about her for which I was thankful. I had given it to her for her fortieth birthday when I was eight years old. It ended with an apology for not making it to forty.

"It was the way you described the things that was so good about it. You have a way with words. You're funny. It made me cry."

She wants to know what my book is about. I tell her it's a memoir about something that has been on my mind lately. I can't bring myself to tell her. I know how I'd feel if Max or Maddie went through what I did. I'm worried I'll break her heart.

Dad comes home. He wants to wash his hands before he handles the phone.

There are three phones in their house. One of them is older than me.

He picks it up, but the static and crackling make it impossible to hear him. He goes upstairs to pick up the other landline, which is almost as old as me. More crackling, more static.

He hangs up that phone, but I'm still on the line with Mom. I hear them yelling through the house to each other.

"You hang up," he shouts.

"Okay, but you have to pick up again before I do or else we'll disconnect."

"Okay."

Dad picks up, there is more crackling and static and then the line clears.

"Hey, Karin! How ya doin'?"

"Happy Father's Day, Dad!"

He says thank you. We talk about the puzzle I sent him. The picture is of a stained-glass rooster. Jeff, Maddie, Max and I did the same one a few months ago and enjoyed it. I thought he'd like it too. We talk about the chipmunk traps. I accuse him of planning to murder Chip and Dale. He concedes chipmunks are cute, and it's an unfortunate bit of business, but when they make their way into your garage, get into your vehicles and start chewing on wires, you've got to take a stand. We talk about how Steve called him earlier, how my sister brought them pizza and salad the night before, how Dave and his wife, Pam, are coming over for a BBQ later. We talk about how because of the COVID-19 pandemic, it will probably be a long time before I can come visit them.

We end our talk the way we always do.

"I love you, Karin. Your mom and I think about you all the time."

"I love you too, Dad."

I take a shower. The hum of the fan and the flow of the water empties my mind and as I massage coconut-scented shampoo into my scalp, a vision pops into my head and my knees buckle. It's a vision of my dad, sitting in his armchair at home. The most comfortable chair with the most awful orange and brown striped upholstery. The chair all of us kids fought to sit it in, making sure to shout, "Save seat!" if we needed to get up to pee or make a snack, lest it be commandeered before we return. The chair that, when having a friend over, we sat in and made them sit in Mom's stilted and jarring rocker. The chair from which we were all summarily evicted when Dad decided to sit.

Dad is sitting in that chair, relaxed, reading his newspaper when suddenly he hears something, something startling. Alert, he raises his head and sees something, something that registers a mixture of shock, concern, and anger on his face. Something that causes him to instinctually spring into action. It's a look and a jump I've seen before as he sprang into action to slap a rogue firework off of my nana's lap on the Fourth of July, sprinted round the dinner table when one of us was choking, leapt to catch us when we fell.

And now I see him as he jumps out of his chair. I feel him pull the boy off me as if the boy weighs nothing. Puts himself between me and the boy. Gives the boy a look that shrivels the smile off of his face, turns the laughter in his throat to dust. Then Dad turns to the teacher and with his arm firmly around my shoulder, not letting me out of sight, out of his protection, he has a conversation. And the teacher has nothing to counter, nothing to defend, because what happened to me was wrong, and I didn't deserve it and it wasn't my fault.

Standing there in the shower, my tears mixing with shampoo and water, I know I never need to ask my dad what he would have done.

I finish my shower, dry off and brush out my hair, which has grown past my shoulders. I open my closet. All of the Eddie Bauer packages are gone. I returned them over a month ago and haven't bought anything since.

I pick out something to wear, get dressed and look in the mirror. My outfit's not quite right. I think of Val, smile, keep it on and sit down at my computer. I document my dreams, my walk, my conversation with my parents, my vision. I already know it will be my last chapter, but I'm not ready to write it yet. I'm still working on chapter eight. Jeff reads each chapter as I finish it. I know when he's read one because he'll come stand in my doorway, look at me sadly, and open his arms to invite me in to be comforted. I try to explain to him that what he read isn't me. That I'm no longer chapter one or five or eight. I am not her. *Now is not then.*

The change is hard for him to gauge because to all outward appearances I look the same and act the same: because for all of my adult life I practised looking and acting like the person I thought I was supposed to be. The person I wanted to be. The difference now is that I'm finally starting to feel like that person, and that feeling outshines my past. And even though the past is still there, and it seemed like everything while I was in it, I don't feel like I live there or breathe that air.

It doesn't mean I won't go there again. I will most certainly fall into my old shadows or be overcome by new ones. My heart will pound. My mind will race. My neck will twitch. My walls will go up. I will choke on the gloomy air. I will pace the mall. But I will also be able to recognize it, and see it for what it is, and I will know how to find my way back.

RESOURCES

Below are some of the books, online courses, websites, and videos I have mentioned in this book or have since used and found to be helpful.

TRAUMA RESOURCES

BOOKS

Edmund J. Bourne, PhD. *The Anxiety and Phobia Workbook*. New Harbinger Publications; Seventh Edition, Revised (May 2020)

The Anxiety and Phobia Workbook is filled with information and tools for recognizing, assessing and treating anxiety and phobias. While the title does not specify trauma, it does include information and recommendations for PTSD. Many of the tools I use and mention in my book are included in the workbook, including relaxation training, cognitive therapy (the dreaded triangle), and affirmations (mantras). The Personal Bill of Rights I refer to came from this workbook. While I did not have this book during the period my memoir covers, I have since bought it, found it to be an invaluable resource, and believe much of the information, recommendations and skills taught are helpful for mental health healing and general mental health fitness.

Peter A. Levine, PhD, with Ann Frederick. *Waking the Tiger: Healing Trauma*. North Atlantic Books; Illustrated edition (July 1997)

Waking the Tiger was the first book I read about trauma after my first meeting with Val. It helped me understand what the effects of trauma are on a person's body and mind without focusing on whether or not the event that caused it meets a defined threshold to be called a traumatic experience. It also gave me hope that as dooming as the word *trauma* sounds, that not only is trauma treatable, but it is also possible to come out more resilient than before, which is how I now feel. I believe practising Levine's exercises outlined in this book, as well as the ones in his online course which I mention below, were instrumental in helping unlock my unresolved trauma.

Ellen Bass and Laura Davis. *The Courage to Heal: A Guide for Women Survivors of Child Sexual Abuse*. William Morrow Paperbacks; 4th -20th Anniversary edition (November 2008)

The pages my therapist gave me are from *The Courage to Heal*. I did not read the rest of this book so I cannot make a recommendation on it. I did, however, find the photocopies from the section "Coping: Honoring What You Did to Survive" extremely helpful in identifying how my sexual assaults may have had an effect on my life. The exercise, along with the authors' recommendation to honour my coping methods, helped me to make peace with and give my past self compassion and understanding.

ONLINE COURSES

www.soundstrue.com/products/
the-healing-trauma-online-course

This is an online course by Peter Levine, the author of *Waking the Tiger,* mentioned above. There is some overlap in information between the book and the course, but the course provides a step-by-step guide in learning about and practising somatic experiencing.

www.pspnet.ca

This is the online program I participated in through Saskatchewan Health. It is only offered to Public Safety Personal and their significant others in certain provinces in Canada. However, the website has self-assessment tools and a resources page that are open to the public and worth checking out. If you are a first responder or a partner of one and live in a province where it is available, I highly recommend taking this course. I believe the mental health skills taught in this course are invaluable to maintaining mental health fitness and recovering from occupational stress injuries.

RESOURCES TO SUPPORT HEALING AND WELL-BEING

BOOKS

Kristen Neff, PhD, and Christopher Germer, PhD. *The Mindful Self-Compassion Workbook*. The Guilford Press; Illustrated edition (August 2018)

The Mindful Self-Compassion Workbook is a step-by-step guide which includes information and concepts about MSC followed by exercises, informal practices and meditations. The authors state MSC is a proven way to accept yourself and build inner strength. I purchased and completed this workbook approximately one year after my memoir ends. True to the authors' claims, I became more accepting of myself and more resilient. I still practise MSC on a semi-regular basis or when I need a dose of self-compassion. It has helped me be a kinder and more supportive friend to myself and I believe (and hope) to others.

Rick Hanson, PhD. *Hardwiring Happiness: The New Brain Science of Contentment, Calm and Confidence.* Harmony (October 2013)

I read and used the practices described in *Hardwiring Happiness* about two years after my memoir ends. In the book Hanson describes the brain's negativity bias and offers suggestions and practices to counterbalance it. The practices are simple, short and, in my experience, very effective. While the title suggests it will make a person happier, the subtitle, *The New Brain Science of Contentment, Calm and Confidence,* in my opinion, is a more accurate description of what a person can expect from practising the exercises. I use the exercises on a semi-regular basis or when I need a dose of contentment, calm or confidence.

WEBSITES

https://positivepsychology.com/self-worth/

This is the website I mention in my memoir. It is free and worth checking out.

https://self-compassion.org/

This is the website of Dr. Kristen Neff, one of the authors of *The Mindful Self-Compassion Workbook,* mentioned above. It offers information about self-compassion as well as self-compassion practices.

https://chrisgermer.com/

This is the website of Dr. Christopher Germer, one of the authors of *The Mindful Self-Compassion Workbook,* mentioned above. It offers information about his 8-week online or in-person MSC course as well as a section with free MSC meditations and practices.

RESOURCES TO SUPPORT SEXUAL HEALING

BOOKS

Wendy Maltz. *The Sexual Healing Journey: A Guide for Survivors of Sexual Abuse*. William Morrow Paperbacks; 3rd Revised, Updated edition (June 2012)

Maltz's book not only helped me to understand my unhelpful thoughts, feelings, and behaviours about sex, it also informed me what healthy sexuality looks like. The book is filled with information, assessments, and practices that assisted me (with the help of my partner, Jeff) with beginning to heal sexually. The practices are deceptively simple and may even seem silly, but I found them worthwhile. Watching the videos listed below was also helpful.

ONLINE VIDEOS

Wendy Maltz — *Partners In Healing* — YouTube: https://www.youtube.com/watch?v=sIRi8F9gCI8

Wendy Maltz — *Relearning Touch* — YouTube: https://www.youtube.com/watch?v=KXE14sDPOP8&t=4s

MEDITATIONS TO SUPPORT HEALING

I meditate semi-regularly most of the time and more when I feel I need it. My sweet spot for meditation is twenty minutes but I find that any time devoted to meditation is helpful. There are tons of meditations available for free online. These are the ones I use regularly.

Compassionate Body Scan — 20 Minute Guided Meditation — YouTube: https://www.youtube.com/watch?v=OS_iqfGjL78

Body scans have been very useful for me to bridge the mind back to the body and teach it that the body is a safe place to be. Body scans are my go-to meditation.

Self-Compassion Break (Audio Meditation) — YouTube: https://www.youtube.com/watch?v=T_80y_CT32c

I try to remember to use a self-compassion break whenever I am feeling frustrated, angry, hurt, disappointed or overwhelmed with a situation or am being particularly hard or critical about myself.

Affectionate Breathing (Audio Meditation) — YouTube: https://www.youtube.com/watch?v=3EfTOL6Regw

This is a nice mindfulness meditation.

Loving Kindness for Beginners (Audio Meditation) — YouTube: https://www.youtube.com/watch?v=QG-CsHbkkzE

I like to include loving kindness meditations like this one in my practice. It helps me foster more kindness for myself and others.

RESOURCES THAT HELPED ME OVERCOME MY BODY IMAGE AND FOOD AND EXERCISE ISSUES

WEBSITES

Embrace: The Documentary — Body Image Movement: https://bodyimagemovement.com/embrace/embracethedocumentary/

Embrace, the documentary by Taryn Brumfitt, explores what she calls the world-wide epidemic of body hating and offers an alternative: body acceptance. Watching this documentary was the catalyst to my decision to stop hating my body, continual body-checking and trying to make it ever smaller through obsessive calorie counting and over-exercising.

BOOKS

Evelyn Tribole, MS, RDN, and Elyse Resch, MS, RDN, FADA. *Intuitive Eating: A Revolutionary Anti-Diet Approach*. St. Martin's Griffin; 3rd edition (August 2012)

Intuitive Eating is filled with information and advice which runs counter to the prevailing diet culture that kept me trapped in an unhealthy relationship with food. Following the advice in this book helped me to honour and trust my hunger cues and make peace with food.

Linda Bacon, PhD. *Health at Every Size: The Surprising Truth About Your Weight*. BenBella Books; 2nd edition (May 2010).

In this book, Dr. Bacon uses research and studies to counter the thin is equal to healthy narrative prevalent in society. Dr. Bacon's objective is to help people be and feel healthy at any size. Instead of trying to control the body at all costs through diet and exercise, Dr. Bacon advises people to tune in and trust their bodies and to give their bodies the food and movement that feels good for them.

Linda Bacon, PhD, and Lucy Aphramor, PhD. *Body Respect: What Conventional Health Books Leave Out, Get Wrong, and Just Plain Fail to Understand About Weight*. BenBella Books; 1st edition (September 2014)

This book supports and builds on Dr. Bacon's book, *Health at Every Size*, listed above. It promotes Health At Every Size (HAES) principles, body respect and body positivity. Both books not only helped me to treat myself and my body with more kindness and respect, they also helped me to shed my judgement about people whose shapes and sizes do not line up with traditional societal standards of health and beauty.

FURTHER READING

June Larkin. *Sexual Harassment: High School Girls Speak Out.*
Second Story Press (November 1994)

Written by a former teacher, *High School Girls Speak Out* lays
out in detail the regular and routine sexual harassment teenage
girls are exposed to and the long-term effects. Reading this book
was challenging, as I recognized how many of the examples of
sexual harassment took place in my own school, where it was
minimized, overlooked, and accepted. I believe this should be
required reading for every school administrator, teacher, parent
and student.

ACKNOWLEDGEMENTS

I want to thank:

My therapist, Val. This book would not have been possible without your insight, guidance and compassion. You made all the difference in my life. Words cannot express…

My husband, Jeff, who, after reading each chapter, said, "It's got good bones. Keep going." Thank you for always being on my side and in my corner. I love you. Always.

My children, Maddie and Max, who had nothing to do with the writing of this book but everything to do with keeping life interesting, fun, and full of love while I was writing it. I love you both more than you can ever imagine.

My friend, Marina Endicott, and my first editor, Glenda MacFarlane, who believed in this book and advocated for me in the publishing world. Thank you both for cheerleading me to the finish.

My publisher and editor, Karen Haughian, who took a chance on a complete unknown in the writing world. Thank you for your keen editorial insight and all the weekends you worked to make this book happen.

My friends and family who were my readers and supporters: Tillen, Rod, Norlane, Jill, Mirjana, Christen, Steve, Pam, Trudy, Tina, Lisa, Carly, and Char. Thank you for your feedback and encouragement. It meant the world to me.

And finally, deepest thanks to my mom and dad, who always encouraged my writing and who, when I finally told them what this book was about, were heartbroken for me, told me they would have helped me and then sent me a pair of Wonder Woman socks because they believe I am a warrior. I love you both. So very much.

A Canadian transplant from the American Midwest, Karin Martel makes her home in Saskatoon, Saskatchewan with her partner, Jeff. While homeschooling their children, Maddie and Max, she worked part-time writing for the documentary series *Legend Hunters, Injustice* and *100 Saskatchewan Stories*. Her non-fiction has been published in *Spring Magazine*. After being fired from her teaching position by her children, Karin changed gears and became a Special Constable with the Saskatoon Police Service, where she worked for thirteen years as a 911 operator, police call-taker and police dispatcher. She is currently serving as the SPS ViCLAS Coordinator, a position which requires her to read and document every sexual assault reported to the Saskatoon Police. Karin currently writes non-fiction related to her memoir *Shop Class Hall Pass*. When she runs out of things to say about that, she'll move on to fiction.

Eco-Audit
Printing this book using Rolland Enviro100 Book
instead of virgin fibres paper saved the following resources:

Trees	Water	Air Emissions
3	1,000 L	165 kg